HOW TO TALK MONEY

HOW TO TALK MONEY

by
Dianna B. Crowe

Introduction by
James K. Glassman

World Almanac Publications
New York, New York

Interior design: Clare Ultimo
Cover design: Lawrence Ratzkin

First published in 1984.

Paperback edition distributed in the United States by Ballantine Books,
a division of Random House, Inc. and in Canada by Random House of Canada, Ltd.

Library of Congress Catalog Card Number: 84-050705
Newspaper Enterprise Association ISBN 0-911818-57-X
Ballantine Books ISBN 0-345-31709-2

Printed in the United States of America.
World Almanac Publications
Newspaper Enterprise Association
A division of United Media Enterprises
A Scripps-Howard Company
200 Park Avenue
New York, NY 10166

INTRODUCTION BY JAMES K. GLASSMAN

resh from a three-martini lunch, a well-dressed woman carrying a Louis Vuitton bag walked into a fur store in midtown Manhattan. She smiled at the salesman and asked him to show her a mink coat.

He brought out one without a price tag and told her it cost $8,000. Nice, she said, but do you have something better? The manager had overheard the exchange, and he moved closer. The salesman brought out another mink. He was about to tell her it cost $12,000 when the manager leaned over to him and said, "Ocean it, Bob."

"This coat," said the salesman, "is $15,000 and worth every penny." The woman said fine, wrote out a check for $15,000, and walked out of the store wearing the coat for which another, less obviously well-heeled customer would have paid $3,000 less.

"Ocean it"?

In the fur business, that bit of jargon means to apply an

"o.c.," or an overcharge, to the normal price of the coat—because the customer looks hot, looks like she'll pay more than the regular price.

If the woman had known the term, she might have saved $3,000.

The jargon of the fur trade is, of course, beyond the scope of this book. But you'll find terms here that will be even more profitable to know. And, while it's doubtful that most of us will ever find phrases like "ocean it" popping up in our daily lives, it's clear that knowing financial jargon today is a necessity.

The Great Investing Game, and Why We All Have to Play It

I like investing. I like ups and downs of markets. I like waking up every morning and finding that the markets have assigned new values to things: General Motors is up three-eighths, the prime rate has fallen a quarter, gold is worth $3.25 more per ounce. I find the bidding, the winning, and the losing to be among life's great pleasures.

But I can understand that not everyone gets his kicks this way.

In happier times—say, before 1970—you could decide yourself whether you wanted to play the Great Investing Game. If you didn't like it, you didn't have to participate. You could stash your nest egg away in government bonds or utility stocks and not think about the money until you retired—and there it was, waiting for you, worth a good deal more than when you stashed it. If you had a few hundred dollars left in your checking account at the end of the month, you could put it in a savings passbook. Or buy U.S. savings bonds.

These transactions fell under the rubric of "personal finance." They weren't part of the deep, fast, mysterious world of investing and speculating—of what they did on Wall Street and in the trading rooms of giant banks. You didn't have to know the prime lending rate, or the federal funds rate, or even what the phrase "money market" meant. Things were simple.

Today, there's no choice. Practically everyone has to play the game. Inflation, high taxes, and the extreme volatility of the economy have made investments that used to be considered safe suddenly very risky. People who stashed $10,000 away several years ago in government bonds have seen the value of their investment reduced by half. Some utility companies have come close to bankruptcy, and some of the biggest have taken the unprecedented step of skipping their dividends. And passbook savings accounts? Today, these old standbys are an outright gyp, for people who simply don't know that they can get far higher rates (with the same liquidity and the same low risk) in money-market accounts and certificates of deposit.

The First and Most Important Step: Learning the Language

Like it or not, you're being dealt into the Great Investment Game. And it's clear that the first and most important step is learning the nomenclature. Before you can decide where to put your money and for how long, you have to understand the language of money. This book will teach you. Read it straight through from the start, or plunge in anywhere you want. Or use it strictly as a reference work: When you come across a word or a phrase you don't know in a financial article in a newspaper or in conversation with a saavy investor, look it up here.

This is the age of financial anxiety. The ground has become shaky. The eternal verities aren't eternal anymore. Worst of all, there seems to be no one to whom to turn for answers.

And that's where this book comes in. It provides something more than edification. It provides comfort. The fact is that in the financial world, a little knowledge can be a wonderful thing. You don't need a degree in business administration or seven years as a stockbroker to understand investing. What you need is a sense of the language, an eye that can recognize terms that often mystify or mislead, translate them into English, and marshal them in common-sense analysis.

This book demystifies financial jargon. Read it, and you'll learn that:

● Prime is not merely the most expensive cut of meat.

● A red herring isn't just an appetizer you eat with sour cream.

● The daily gold fix doesn't refer to shooting up with expensive drugs.

Read this book and you'll learn that LIFO is different from FIFO, a little fact that could keep you from investing in a stock-market loser that's decked out to look like a winner.

You'll be able to tell a g.o. (general obligation) municipal bond from a revenue bond, and you'll quickly see why revenue bonds are usually far more risky. You'll be able to distinguish between Ginnie Mae and Fannie Mae, and you'll find out what makes them different from their cousin

Freddie Mac. You'll learn how Regulation A differs from Regulation Q. You'll be able to make sense of strange terms like rehypothecation and zero uptick.

Most of all, by using this book, you'll manage to avoid being a lamb: an inexperienced, unsophisticated investor with little knowledge of the investment world.

You'll be able to talk to investment professionals—some of whom like nothing more than shearing lambs—with confidence. You'll get the attention and the advice that you deserve. Or, if you prefer, you'll be able to handle most of your personal financial needs yourself.

Putting Your Financial House In Order

What are most of us anxious about when it comes to money? It's not the federal deficit, or the balance of payments problem, or the Federal Reserve's open-market policy. What strikes terror in most of our hearts is the disorder of our own financial houses. We worry about getting the kids through college, how we'll provide for our own retirement, how we'll ever be able to afford a home (or a vacation home) of our own, how we'll pay the Christmas bills. How can you put your own financial house in order? I'll give you some advice below, but first, it's important to understand why the financial scene today has become so complicated, why you're feeling a bit bewildered. And why you have to learn the game, its rules, and its terminology.

The Economy

Back in the good old days—say, between 1952 and 1974—prices were relatively stable and the economy was relatively serene. During that period, inflation generally ran at 2 to 3 percent; it hit 6 percent only once, in

1970. Between 1952 and 1974, there were four recessions, but none lasted more than a year. But from 1974 to 1984, consumer prices have fluctuated wildly, peaking at over 10 percent three times; meanwhile, we've had three recessions, two of them lasting more than a year.

To the small investor, this kind of uncertainty is disastrous. Look, for example, at three-month Treasury bills, usually a safe and stable investment. During a single year (1980) T-bills started off paying more than 15 percent, then plummeted to below 7 percent, then, before year's end, hit 15 percent again.

Then there's the stock market. Adjusted for inflation, the Dow-Jones Industrial Average was lower at the start of 1984 than it was in 1955, even though in nominal terms, it was 300 percent higher.

And consider whole-life insurance. Not too long ago, it was a sensible investment. It gave your family a substantial sum if you died and accumulated a decent cash value as well. Today, most whole-life policies are a bad joke. A death benefit that sounded enormous ten or twenty years ago (for instance, $100,000 or $200,000) is simply inadequate for many families today. And the effective interest rate on the investment portion of a whole-life policy in recent years has been tiny compared with other vehicles.

If the economy over the past decade has wreaked such havoc that you can't trust government bonds or blue-chip stocks or conservative life-insurance policies, what can you do? Well, you can try one of the fancy new "products" that Wall Street is churning out by the minute: unit trusts, index futures, tax exempt money-market funds. Confused? You're not alone.

Taxes

Not too many years ago, most middle-class and even upper-middle-class Americans didn't have to worry about taxes. Sure, we paid them, but we were in low enough brackets that we didn't have to consider the virtues of oil-drilling partnerships or highly leveraged real estate deals, or to ponder going into debt up to our ears to get some extra deductions. Now, thanks to the effect of inflation on the progressive tax system, the majority of Americans do have to worry about taxes—worry a lot. And worrying about taxes means having to learn about sophisticated investments.

For example, despite the Reagan tax cuts of the early 1980s, someone fresh out of law school taking a job with a decent-sized firm would probably do well to put a little money into municipal bonds. Ten or fifteen years ago, tax-free bonds were what senior partners bought just before their retirement. New lawyers put whatever they could into a savings account so that someday they could afford a house.

Everyone who's in a tax bracket of 30 percent or higher (or plans to be) should take taxes into account in making investment, insurance, and retirement decisions. That category includes the vast majority of Americans. And I don't have to remind you of the complexity of the IRS code. To understand its vagaries can be a lifetime pursuit.

Financial Institutions

Ten years ago, if you needed advice on stocks and bonds, you knew just where to go: to a stockbroker. Today, you can go to a savings and loan association or to a department store. But it has to be the right S & L or the right department store (Sears owns Dean Witter Reynolds). Now, you could go to a bank to execute stock trades, but banks aren't allowed to give advice on stocks, so they operate discount brokerages.

Banking? Some of the best deals on checking accounts come from mutual fund houses in Boston or Minneapolis. Home mortgage loans? CIT Financial was soliciting them the other day with a stuffer in the daily newspaper—the way Zayre solicits pajama-buyers. Insurance? You can go practically anywhere: to brokers, banks, S & Ls, financial planners, or, again, to Sears. But not everyone is allowed to sell every kind of insurance.

The era of the financial supermarket is dawning.

Selling many financial products under one roof may sound on the surface as exciting and as practical as a supermarket displacing butchers and produce shops by selling meat and vegetables under one roof. But it's not so simple. Today's financial supermarkets don't sell *everything* under one roof; the regulators won't let them. It's as though the government said that some stores can sell meat and fruit and others can sell chicken and vegetables, but that no store can sell meat and vegetables or chicken and fruit.

And there's another problem: The employees of these new financial supermarkets (some of which are literally supermarkets—you can do your banking and your grocery shopping at Public stores in Florida and in other similar chains around the country) can't keep up with the new products. It's tough enough for a stockbroker to follow a few thousand stocks. Now he's supposed to be an expert on commodities, insurance, and money-market funds. "It will be hard to train someone how to sell 149 different products," says Michael O. Sanderson, vice president and group manager of the Cash Management Group at Merrill Lynch, "but we are involved in an on-going effort to do just that."

Someday, financial supermarkets will function smoothly and efficiently, but that day has not yet arrived. Today, with federal regulations changing by the minute, mergers and consolidations have made getting help from financial institutions more confusing. Not less.

Take Your Pick: Anxiety or Apathy

The economic storms of the 1970s and 1980s have produced two seemingly contradictory responses in most people:

• Acute anxiety. We worry how we'll ever meet our obligations to ourselves and our family.

• Severe apathy. With the financial scene so complicated, we have an impulse to walk away from tough decisions. We shrug at impending problems, and we hope that something will turn up.

Neither of these responses—and many families alternate between them—is useful. They serve as excuses, ways to help us avoid looking at the facts. And the main fact is that we all have to play the Great Investment Game, like it or not. So we might as well try to like it.

What should you do? There are two alternatives, and, whichever you choose, it's vital that you understand how to talk money.

Secrets of Getting Professional Financial Help

The first choice is to get professional help, which sounds simple in theory but turns out to be difficult in practice. The problem is that, unless you're very rich and can afford a financial adviser who charges $100 to $200 an hour, you'll have to get help from someone who makes his living through commissions on the investments that he sells you. Most financial counsellors are employed by insurance companies, mutual fund houses, or brokerage firms, and their livelihoods depend on pushing the products of their employers. You may run across intelligent, altruistic planners working for, say, an insurance company, but they're not likely to tell you you're overinsured.

Can you overcome this kind of bias? Yes, but it's not easy.

You'll have to learn some financial basics. And one good way to start is by taking an inventory of your assets and liabilities and a look at your sources of income and your expenses. Make a list of what you have and what you owe. Do a rough budget, listing your income and outgo. Many financial counsellors provide questionnaires to guide you in taking this sort of inventory. If you have enough confidence to go to such an advisor and ask for a questionnaire without committing yourself further, then do so.

The important thing is that you yourself understand the assets and liabilities that you own. And, here, this book comes in very handy. I remember, for example, applying for my first loan. I was starting a small business, and the loan officer looked down my meager balance sheet and spotted something he liked. "Here's something we can use for collateral," he said. "You've got a C.D. here. When does it mature?"

I was baffled. I didn't know what "collateral" meant, much less "C.D." I had a vague idea about "mature," but I was afraid to show my general ignorance. I managed to bluff my way through the interview, but I nearly made the kind of mistake that could have cost me the loan. The bank officer could easily have reasoned, "If this guy doesn't know what's on his own balance sheet, how can I trust him with the bank's hard-earned cash?"

So if you own stock in a closed-end investment company, or if you have $10,000 in certificates of deposit, or if you have a bunch of stock options in the company you work for, you're well advised to look up the puzzling terms in this book—to get acquainted with the basics of your financial life.

Then, armed with this knowledge, you can approach financial advisors—even biased ones—and make your own decision on how much they can help you.

Doing It Yourself

You may decide, after interviewing a few planners, that you can set your financial house in order just as well yourself. If you choose the do-it-yourself route, you'll still probably be using professionals to help you purchase the investments you want to make, but the selections will be mainly yours. Here's some advice on how to go about it.

1. Examine your expenses carefully.

This is the vital first step. It's not very exciting; in fact, it may be excruciatingly painful. But it has to be done. The object is to pare down your spending enough to be able

11

to set aside something for savings each month—ideally 5 to 7 percent of your take-home income.

Most people find that if they don't force themselves to save, the money gets quickly spent. The best idea is simply to make a deposit to your savings program at the same time you receive your paycheck. The benefits are obvious. For example, if you can manage to stash away $480 a month in a money-market fund paying 10 percent interest, you will accumulate $100,000 after ten years, which should be enough to send a child to a top college (assuming inflation averages 6 to 8 percent annually).

Deciding what you want to spend your money on is your own business. Some people simply can't function without a month's vacation in Europe every year, and they're willing to live modestly the remaining eleven months to be able to afford it. My point is only that savings has to be a major priority; savings can't be whatever is left over after the trip to the Europe and the new car and the expensive nights out.

2. Build an emergency reserve.

Why save? The main reason is to build an easily accessible store of money to meet expenses in an emergency—for example, in case you come down with a serious illness not covered by insurance, or if you or your spouse is out of work. The reserve should be earning interest, and it should be liquid ("an asset or other investment that can easily be converted into cash"). The most obvious place to keep your reserve is in a money-market fund or its equivalent at a bank or savings-and-loan.

How much should you set aside? Most financial experts suggest one or two months' salary.

Some people feel safer keeping their emergency reserve in a passbook savings or even in a checking account. This is foolish. Many money-market funds invest solely in government-insured instruments (you'll find definitions for any mystifying terms here later in the book). And banks frequently offer money-market accounts that pay nearly twice the interest that passbook accounts do, and both are insured by the same agency of the federal government.

3. Start saving for a large purchase.

We all covet things we can't afford. Until the tax laws (and perhaps our own changing mores) turned Americans into voracious borrowers, making both major and minor purchases on credit, most of us traditionally saved until we could get what we wanted: a house, a car, a trip to Europe, a college education for our kids. The Tax Code remains biased against saving (income produced from investments is taxed at high rates) and in favor of borrowing (interest is deductible and inflation enables you to pay off the loans in cheaper dollars).

But saving for a large purchase hasn't gone out of style—nor should it. Many people simply can't tolerate the burden of debt. They don't sleep well at night. And many large purchases still require a large cash down payment—houses come to mind.

For this kind of saving, you can probably tolerate a little more risk and a little less liquidity than for your emergency reserve. Corporate bonds might be a good idea, or, if you're in a high enough tax bracket (40 percent and up), tax-free municipal bonds may make sense. To spread the risk, you can buy into a unit investment trust. What's that? Just look under "U": "A diversified portfolio of income securities, for example, corporate bonds, municipal bonds, or preferred stocks, which are pooled and sold to investors in the form of units. Each unit represents a fractional undivided interest in both the principal and income of the portfolio." In other words, instead of buying just one bond, you can buy little bits of many bonds.

4. Plan for your retirement.

The tax bias against saving vanishes if the saving is for retirement. The Tax Code now allows practically anyone to open an Individual Retirement Account (IRA), usually with a bank, savings-and-loan association, investment firm, or insurance company. If you're self-employed you can get a similar break with a Keogh plan. The amount you invest each year is tax-deductible, so by making a $2,000 investment, someone in a 40 percent bracket can cut his taxes by $800. Actually tax-deferred is a better phrase. When you retire and withdraw the money from your IRA or Keogh, you'll have to pay taxes on the investment, but the rate will probably be lower than during your working years.

More important, the income that your IRA investment generates isn't taxable at all before you withdraw it. That income keeps compounding untaxed at a high rate. And the results of this compounding can be astonishing. For example, if you put $2,000 a year into an IRA that earns 8 percent annually, you'll have $227,000 at the end of 30 years. If your IRA earns 12 percent, you'll have $714,000.

Almost everyone should have an IRA. It even makes sense to make contributions to your account if (1) you think you might need the money in a few years, or (2) you don't have cash on hand. Even if you need your IRA money, the penalty for early withdrawal is not so great. In many cases, it's cancelled out within five years by the advantage of untaxed compound interest. And, if you're short of cash, then borrow.

IRAs and Keoghs aren't the only provision for your retirement. There's Social Security, of course, and perhaps your company retirement plan. But, in many cases, these sources together account for less than half of a couple's pre-retirement income. Is that enough to live on? It could be, but I wouldn't count on Social Security benefits being as generous in ten or twenty years as they are today. So take advantage of one of the few tax breaks the middle class can exploit: Open an IRA or a Keogh.

Where should you put your retirement account money? The best idea is to spread it around. Put part in a money-market fund or bank equivalent, part in stock mutual funds, part in a bond fund. Remember, however, that the great advantage is the non-taxability of the income that your investment is throwing off. So make sure it throws some income off. In other words, an IRA invested in a bond fund that's earning 10 percent in interest a year probably makes more sense than an IRA invested in high-growth stocks that don't pay dividends.

5. Invest for fun and profit.

Now we get to the good stuff. Once you've settled on your financial plan and made investments that will take care of such necessities as retirement, you can have your fun. Go into real estate tax shelters, buy orange-juice contracts on the futures market, sell options on stock you don't own. Investing—for those who don't mind the risk— can be profitable and exciting.

And, if you are as fascinated with investing as I am, you'll find this book endlessly rewarding. You'll plunge into such exotica as stop-limit orders and straddles, blind pool partnerships and blue lists, flower bonds and forward markets.

But, best of all, there is the stock market—the shares of thousands of companies, up for bids, changing every day. Warren Buffett, one of the most successful stock-market investors of our time, describes investing as the only business in which you can sit waiting for the pitch you like. You can wait all day, all year, before you swing. If you own a chain of shoe stores, for instance, and a competitor opens a store five miles out of town, you're forced to play your hand: Open a store to compete with him (and probably lose money for several years) or concede the suburban market. You have to pick—you have to swing. But investing is different. If you don't like the price of General Electric today, you can wait until tomorrow. Or check out General Foods or General Motors or General Dynamics or General Mills or General Host.

In investing, the choices are practically infinite, the action constant. And this book will help you play a challenging and rewarding game that's become more than a game. Dig in. Enjoy it.

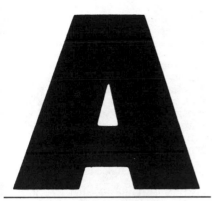

above par: At a premium, a price greater than face amount or par value. *Compare* below par, discount.

accelerated depreciation: IRS-approved depreciation methods that allow for a greater than normal rate of depreciation in early years on an asset because the actual economic life of the asset is considered to be shorter than its physical life. This allowance can stimulate economic growth by giving rapid cost recovery for tax purposes.

account: *See* brokerage account.

account balance: The net difference between all credits and debits in the brokerage account.

account executive: A registered representative of a broker-dealer firm who is licensed in accordance with SEC and state regulations to handle security transactions for investors. Though often just called broker or stockbroker, the preferred terms are registered representative or account executive.

accounts payable: The sums owed by business entities to creditors which are due and payable in one year or less.

accounts receivable: The claims of business entities against their debtors which are to be received within one year or less.

accretion: An increase in value made monthly for tax and accounting purposes to adjust the purchase price of an original-issue discounted bond so that the acquisition price will equal par value at maturity. *Compare* amortization.

accrued: An accumulated increase or decrease. A claim earned or incurred but not yet received or paid.

accrued interest: Pro rata interest that has accumulated for the benefit of the holder of an instrument since the last interest payment date. In bond transactions, the buyer normally must pay to the seller the current market price plus accrued interest up to but not including settlement date.

accumulated distribution: Income received by a trust for future distribution. The income is taxed to the beneficiaries in the year in which the trust receives the income rather than when distributed.

accumulation: (1) The absorption of an excess supply of stock by an increasing demand for that stock. This usually has a favorable effect on the market price. Accumulation generally occurs after a price decline when demand becomes dominant. *Compare* distribution. (2) Gradually acquiring shares of a security over a period of time so as to avoid public market attention.

accumulation plan: Various programs available from mutual funds for purchasing additional shares of the fund. These include both contractual and voluntary programs.

acid test: One method used to determine the short-term liquidity of a company. It is calculated by dividing current assets less inventory value by current liabilities. *Also called* quick ratio.

acquisition: To acquire an asset in whole or part, or to gain controlling interest. Most often used to mean the purchase of one company by another.

acquisition cost: In mutual funds, it is the sales charge a client must pay for investment in a specific fund. *Also called* load or front-end load.

across the board: Widespread action. For example, the market prices of most securities in a particular industry increase or decrease at approximately the same time.

acting in concert: The coordination of securities transactions among individuals in a manner which might influence the price of a given security.

active account: Brokerage account in which transactions occur at relatively frequent intervals.

active market: Market in which there is unusually heavy trading. This does not indicate whether the market is up or down, but rather one in which there is a greater than normal number of shares being traded.

activity: The trading volume of a particular stock or group of stocks or the trading volume on a particular exchange for a stated time period.

actual cash value: The value of a contract upon redemption.

actual market: The current market price for a security. The current bid and asked prices for a security.

adjustment: Procedure in which the Options Clearing Corporation adjusts an option contract due to stock splits or stock dividends to maintain, as fairly as possible, the original amount of the contract. Adjustments are not made on option contracts when cash dividend distributions are made.

adjustment bond: *See* income bond.

ADR: Negotiable receipts for certificates of shares of foreign corporations. *See* American depository receipt.

ad valorem tax: Taxation based on the assessed value of property.

advance: To increase in market price or value.

advance/decline index: The cumulative net difference between individual stock prices advancing and those declining for a given period of time. The A/D index is used as a measure of market breadth.

advance/decline ratio: The number of stocks which advanced in price divided by the number of stocks which declined in price for a given time period such as a day or week.

advances versus declines: The number of stocks which closed higher versus the number which closed lower than the previous trading day. Intraday figures are also available.

advancing market: The prevailing trend of the market is rising and generally shows an across-the-board increase in market prices.

advisory service: A service, which, for a fee, gives market information and/or particular buy or sell recommendations to its subscribers.

AE: *See* account executive.

affiliate: A company related to another by owning, being owned, common management, or other direct or indirect control devices.

aftermarket: The auction market which develops for a security after its initial public offering. *Also called* secondary market.

aftertax: The profit or loss received from an investment or business operation after allowing for federal and state taxes.

agency securities: *See* government agency securities.

agent: One who acts on behalf of another. An agent will initiate transactions in the name of the principal and charge a commission for his services. Dealers, on the other hand, buy and sell for their own accounts. *See* broker. *Compare* dealer.

aggregate exercise price: The striking price of an option contract multiplied by the unit of trading of the underlying security covered by the contract.

aggressive portfolio: A portfolio of securities designed for rapid growth of capital rather than income. Greater risk is accepted in hopes of attaining a higher than average return.

agribusiness: Agriculture and agriculture-related businesses that operate on a large scale. This includes production, processing, and distribution.

Alberta Stock Exchange: Address: 300 Fifth Avenue S.W., Calgary, Alberta, Canada T2P 3C4.

allied member: Each partner of a partnership firm that has received a seat on an exchange.

allocation: The established procedure for the issuance of stock option exercise notices by exchange member firms. Allocation procedures are designed to insure fair and nondiscriminatory practices through an approved random-selection process.

all-or-none offering: A public offering of a new security issue in which the entire offering must be sold by a certain date or all offers to buy will be canceled. The underwriter does not purchase the securities in an attempt to resell them, but rather leaves the risk of a successful offering with the issuer.

all-or-none order (AON): Security order to buy or sell with trading instructions (qualifier) that the order must be executed in its entirety or not at all. Partial execution is not acceptable to the investor.

allotment: The number of shares in a new security offering allocated by the underwriter to each firm participating in the distribution.

alternative order: An order to buy or sell with trading instructions (qualifier) that one of two or more alternatives will fill the order and that when one part of the order is executed, the other alternatives are to be automatically canceled.

amalgamation: The consolidation of two or more separate corporations into one single new corporation.

AMBAC: *See* American Municipal Bond Assurance Corporation.

American Bankers Association: Address: 1120 Connecticut Avenue N.W., Washington, D.C. 20036.

American Commodity Exchange: Address: 711 N.E. Third Street, Gresham, Oregon 97030.

American depository receipt (ADR): Receipt for certificates of shares in a foreign corporation. The actual certificates are deposited in a bank and the

ADR is issued in its place. ADRs are negotiable and are used to simplify trading in foreign securities.

American Municipal Bond Assurance Corp. (AMBAC): A corporation that offers insurance policies on new municipal offerings to cover payment of both principal and interest. Bonds covered by this insurance automatically receive the highest bond rating.

American Stock Exchange (AMEX, ASE): The second largest stock exchange in the United States with listing requirements similar to but less stringent than the NYSE. Until 1953 the AMEX was called the New York Curb Exchange. Address: 86 Trinity Place, New York, New York 10006.

American Stock Exchange market value index: Average value of all the common shares listed on the AMEX as well as rights and warrants. This average contains a larger number of growth companies and natural resource companies than the NYSE Index or the Dow Jones Industrial Average.

AMEX: The second largest stock exchange in the United States. *See* American Stock Exchange.

amortization: A decrease in value made monthly for tax and accounting purposes to adjust the price of a bond issued at a premium so that acquisition price will equal par value at maturity. *Compare* accretion.

analyst: Professional in the securities industry who examines and interprets past, present, and projected corporate, economic, and market data in order to make forecasts and recommend investment alternatives. The two main areas of analysis are technical and fundamental.

analyze: To examine and interpret past, present, and projected corporate, economic, and market data and make forecasts based on those findings. The two main areas of analysis are technical and fundamental.

and interest: *See* with interest.

announcement date: The date the corporation announces that a dividend will be paid—stating the record date, payment date, and amount of the dividend. *Also called* declaration date.

annual financial statements: Accounting statements showing income or loss or the financial position of a corporation at the end of the last day of its fiscal year and bearing that date.

annualize: To translate partial figures into an annual rate. Interest is always reported on an annualized basis.

annualized return: The assumed calculated return on an investment over a 12-month period. The annualized return is based on dividends, interest, and possible appreciation.

annual meeting: Yearly meeting at which all stockholders have the privilege of gathering to elect the corporate board of directors and to vote upon certain corporate matters. Generally, few stockholders attend these meetings and instead vote by proxy. The annual meeting is commonly called the stockholders' meeting.

annual report: Corporate yearly statement issued to shareholders and analysts that reports year-end financial information, major developments of the past year, and planned activities for the coming years.

annuitant: One who has been designated recipient of an annuity.

annuity: A sum paid periodically in equal installments to annuitants or their beneficiaries under the terms of an insurance policy or a bequest.

annuity bond: A debt instrument which bears no maturity date and continues to pay interest indefinitely. *Also called* perpetual bond.

anticipation notes: Short-term municipal debt instruments issued to obtain funds in anticipation of revenues or permanent financing. *See* bond anticipation note, revenue anticipation note, and tax anticipation note.

antique: An investment collectible, usually more than 100 years old, which derives its worth from its age, condition, and the current market demand.

appreciation: An increase in value. For example, the increase in the market price of a security.

appreciation potential: The forecasted increase in market value that is projected for an investment. Usually, a market price and percentage of increase is quoted.

approved depository: An exchange-approved bank or trust company in which exchange clearing members may deposit cash, U.S. Treasury bills, letters of credit, or shares of underlying stock in order to meet exchange margin requirements.

approved list: *See* legal list.

arbitrage: The simultaneous purchase and sale of the same or equivalent security on two or more markets to take advantage of a price differential.

arm's length transaction: Transaction in which the parties involved are totally independent of each other. For example, in a securities transaction which takes place through an exchange, the buyer and seller are independent of each other.

arrears: Any amount that is past due. If a bond issuer has not made all interest payments which are due and payable, the interest is in arrears and the bond is in default.

articles of incorporation: Document submitted to the Secretary of State in the state in which a company is seeking incorporation which includes complete information regarding the applying corporation. Once approved and accepted this becomes the corporate charter.

ASE: *See* American Stock Exchange.

asked price: The lowest price that anyone is willing at the current time to accept for a particular security. It is the price a buyer must pay for the security in order to puchase it at that time. *Compare* bid price.

assessment bond: Municipal bond issued for improvements on property under municipal authority, such as sidewalks or drainage, which is retired by property assessment taxes.

asset: Anything of value owned by an individual, estate, or institution. Net assets are the property that remains after all debts have been taken into account.

asset value: *See* net asset value.

assignment: (1) Endorsement of a security certificate by the owner of record to render it negotiable. (2) Notification to the writer of a put or call option contract that the contract has been exercised by the holder (buyer) of that contract. *See* exercise.

associate member: Membership classification used on the American Stock Exchange. These members do not have seats but do have certain privileges of other members.

at market: Instructions given to either buy or sell a security at the current best available price. The order is called a market order.

at-the-close order (CLO): An order to buy or sell a security with trading instructions (qualifier) that the order is to be executed as close to the end of trading of the security for that day as is practical or not at all.

at-the-money: A put or call option for which the strike (exercise) price is equal to the current market value of the underlying security. *Compare* in-the-money, out-of-the-money.

at-the-opening order (OPG): An order to buy or sell a security with trading instructions (qualifier) that the order is to be executed at the opening of trading of the security or not at all. Any portion of the order not executed at the opening will be canceled.

auction market: Market in which buyers compete with other buyers, and sellers compete with other sellers to obtain the best possible price. Securities listed on the various exchanges trade within an auction market system.

authorized capital stock: The maximum number of shares of capital stock that may be issued by a corporation as stated in the articles of incorporation.

Automated Bond System: Computerized system operated by the NYSE that attempts to match all orders for listed nonconvertible bonds.

Automated Pricing and Reporting System: NYSE computer system that processes and assigns a price to qualified odd-lot orders based on the next round-lot sale of that same stock. The transaction information is forwarded to the specialist and the firm presenting the order.

automatic dividend reinvestment: An optional feature offered by most mutual funds which allows for the reinvestment of all income distributions as a means for greater growth over the years.

average: An arithmetic mean, median, or norm which approximately measures a midway value in a set of data.

average down: To reduce the average cost basis of a security by buying more shares of that same security at a lower price.

averages: Single values that represent a set of data. For example, the Dow Jones Bond Average gives the average value of six bond groups and is used to indicate strength or weakness in the bond markets.

average up: To buy more shares of a given security at higher prices than the original purchase price, therefore increasing the average cost basis.

averaging: *See* dollar cost averaging.

BA: *See* banker's acceptance.

baby bond: Any bond issued with a face value of less than $1,000.

back office: The operations department of a brokerage firm. This department handles such activities as record keeping, statements, and margin account requirements.

back up system: The Options Clearing Corporation's settlement procedure that was instituted to insure that members perform their obligations upon assignment of exercised option contracts.

bad delivery: Presenting a security certificate in less than proper form in the completion of a security transaction. *Compare* good delivery.

bail out: Selling securities in a distressed or panicked state with little regard for a possible loss that may be incurred.

balance: (1) The net difference between all debits and credits in an account. (2) The equality of debits and credits in an account.

balanced fund: A mutual fund that invests in many types of securities rather than concentrating on a single kind of security such as municipal bonds.

balance sheet: An accounting statement of the financial position of a company showing all assets, liabilities, and net worth as of a specific date.

BAN: *See* bond anticipation note.

bank: A national- or state-chartered financial organization which lends, holds, and invests money and other instruments of value.

banker's acceptance (BA): A short-term negotiable financial instrument issued by commercial banks and used to finance international trade. It offers an excellent return and a high degree of safety to the investor.

bank guarantee letter: A document issued by an exchange-approved-bank certifying that the bank holds sufficient funds to cover the writing of a put option or that shares are on deposit with the bank to cover the writing of a call option.

bankruptcy: Declared by the courts to be in a state of insolvency and having any assets and all financial matters turned over to a trustee for administration. In some cases, rather than totally dissolving a business, a reorganization or merger is allowed.

bar chart: A price-time axis chart which depicts changes of a stock or a market index and its volume over a period of time. High-low-closing data are usually presented.

barometer stock: Any single issue that moves with economic conditions and is used to verify market changes. Some issues which are used to verify the current state of the market are General Motors, IBM, and Exxon.

Barron's: Highly regarded weekly financial journal. Address: Dow Jones & Co., Inc., 22 Cortland Street, New York, New York 10007.

Barron's Confidence Index: Index that compares yields on high grade bonds against yields on low grade bonds. As yields move down on lower grade bonds, the index reflects an increased confidence in the economy by investors.

base: Charted stock pattern that shows a relatively narrow price range over an extended time span which usually follows a period of decline.

basebuilding: A period of sideways price trend over an extended period of time. It is believed that after a long decline, a basebuilding period is needed before an established price advance can occur.

base period: A period chosen as the point for measuring change in an index. For example, if 1980 were chosen as a base year for a given index, it would be assigned a value of 100; an increase of 10 percent in 1981 would give a price index of 110 for that year.

basis point: Used in measuring yields, 1 basis point equals 1/100 of 1 percent (.01 percent). A yield of 8.10 percent would increase 20 basis points if it moved to 8.30 percent.

bear: One who believes a market or the economy in general will decline. Compare bull.

bearer: The holder and owner of a negotiable instrument. An instrument made payable to bearer may be transferred with delivery—a signature or endorsement is not required.

bearer bond: A bond issued in bearer form rather than being registered in the owner's name. Ownership is determined by possession.

bearish: A negative sentiment regarding a market or the economy with the expectation that market prices will decline. *Compare* bullish.

bear market: A market in which the general trend of security prices is down for a long period of time, several months or more. *Compare* Bull Market.

bear spread: An option strategy in which the investor buys one type of option (either a put or a call) and sells the other on the same underlying security simultaneously. The option that is purchased will have a higher striking price than the one that is sold. The investor expects to profit by a decrease in the market price of the underlying security. Compare bull spread

bear straddle writing: Option writing (selling) strategy involving an uncovered call and a covered put on the same underlying stock at the same striking price with the same expiration date. *Compare* bull straddle writing.

below par: At a discount, a price less than face amount or par value. *Compare* above par.

beneficial interest: A right or interest in something of value such as a trust, insurance policy, or ownership as represented by shares in a corporation or other contract.

beneficiary: The person entitled to receive a benefit from a contractual agreement, such as a trust, life insurance policy, or will.

best efforts offering: Public offering of a new security in which the underwriters agree to use their best efforts in selling the entire issue by a certain date. The underwriter does not buy and then resell the issue but rather leaves the risk with the issuer.

beta: Measure of the average percentage change in the price of a stock or group of stocks relative to that percentage change of a market index over a specific period of time. Generally the higher the beta, the more volatile the stock.

bid and asked: The current spread or quotation for a security. In a quote of 24 to 25, 24 is the bid price and 25 is the asked price. The highest limited price anyone is willing to pay is $24.00 and the lowest limited price to sell is $25.00.

bid price: The highest price that anyone is willing to pay at the current moment for a particular security. It is the price a seller must accept if he wishes to sell his security immediately. *Compare* asked price.

Big Board: Common nickname for the New York Stock Exchange.

Black Tuesday: The day the stock market crashed which was an antecedent to the Great Depression of the 1930s. The date was Tuesday, October 29, 1929.

blind pool partnership: A limited real estate partnership investment in which the assets to be acquired are unknown to the investors at the time of investment.

blind trust: A trust set up in order to protect one from the possibility of a conflict in interest charge in which all financial affairs are handled by a fiduciary.

block: A very large number of shares of a single security—usually 10,000 shares or more.

block transaction: A transaction involving the trade of 10,000 shares or more of a particular stock. Block information is used to measure institutional participation and the liquidity of the market.

blue chip stock: High-grade securities issued by mature companies that are well-established, have great financial strength, and are leaders in their industry. The term is often used to describe the 30 companies listed in the Dow Jones Industrial Average.

Blue List, The: A list published daily of municipal bond offerings throughout the nation. *Also called* Blue Sheets.

blue sky laws: State laws that require registration of securities, dealers, and salespersons and regulate the practices and procedures of those involved in the securities industry within that state.

board: (1) Term applied to the directors of a corporation. (2) Electronic device which displays security trade prices and number of shares traded.

board broker: An exchange member who is registered with an options exchange to act as agent for other brokers and as a principal when trading for his own account.

board of directors: The persons elected by the shareholders of a corporation to serve as the chief policy-making group for corporate affairs.

board of governors: Chief policy-making group of the Federal Reserve System.

board room: (1) Large room open to the public in brokerage offices where latest market prices are quoted on electronic display boards. (2) Place where the board of directors of a corporation meets.

bogus: Counterfeit or otherwise faked or forged.

bond: A debt security issued by a corporation or government unit. It represents a creditor relationship rather than ownership. Most bonds pay a set rate of interest semiannually for the life of the bond with principal due at maturity. Bonds are most often issued in $1,000 units. There are two major classifications of bonds; those in which the interest is fully taxable and those in which the interest is partially or totally tax-free.

bond anticipation note (BAN): A negotiable short-term municipal debt instrument issued in anticipation of permanent financing in the form of a bond issue. The BAN is issued to insure cash flow and is generally retired with the proceeds from the long-term bond issue.

bond discount: The difference between face value and the amount paid for a bond (or current market value) when the acquisition price or current market value is less than face value. On a $1,000 face value bond purchased for $820, the bond discount would be $180.

bond dividend: A rare dividend paid in the form of a bond rather than in cash or additional shares of stock.

bond floor broker: An NYSE member that handles bond transactions in the New York Stock Exchange bond room.

bond fund: A mutual fund investing specifically in corporate bonds in order to achieve high income with safety of principal.

bondholder: The owner of a bond. Bond certificates may be registered in the owner's name or issued in bearer form.

bond house: Securities firm that specializes in handling bond transactions. Their activities normally include underwriting, public offerings, private placement, and handling trades in the secondary market.

bond market: (1) Markets in which bonds are traded. This includes the various exchanges and the over-the-counter market. (2) The actual supply and demand for bonds.

bond premium: The difference between the face value and the amount paid for a bond (or current market value) when the price is greater than face value. On a $1,000 face value bond selling for $1,120, the bond premium is $120.

bond quotations: Corporate bonds are typically issued with face values of $1,000 and quoted in points based on face value. One point equals $10 with minimum variations of 1/8 of a point. For example, ten bonds selling at 92 5/8 would be 10 × 926.25 or $9,262.50.

bond ratings: Systems for evaluating the quality and risks of bonds available for purchase. The most widely recognized firms that rate bonds are Moody's which rates on a scale from Aaa to C and Standard and Poor's which rates from AAA to D.

book: *See* specialist's book.

book value: The theoretical value of a company as carried on the books of the corporation.

book value per share: Calculated by subtracting all liabilities and liquidation value of preferred shares from all assets divided by the number of shares of common stock outstanding. This gives the theoretical per-share book value of a corporation in the event of liquidation.

boom: A period of rapid and strong economic growth that is usually accompanied by a rising stock market.

Boston Stock Exchange: Address: One Boston Place, Boston, Massachusetts 02108.

bottom: Term used to indicate the lowest point that a security price reaches for a given period of time. A bottom must, therefore, be followed by some degree of recovery.

bottom out: Following a period of decline in price, the point where demand for a security starts to exceed supply and a rise in prices will occur.

bourse: Stock exchange. French term used throughout non-English-speaking European countries for stock and commodity exchanges.

box: Term used to indicate a long position, but used especially when referring to an investor selling short while holding his long position.

breadth: (1) The scope and strength of the market direction. Breadth is measured by several indicators including advance/decline and volume figures. Breadth is used to determine major turning points in the market. When advances exceed declines the breadth is considered positive and when declines exceed advances the reverse is true. (2) When referring to a single issue, breadth indicates the extent to which a stock is distributed; that is, the number of shares outstanding and the number of shareholders.

break: A point where security prices begin a definite and strong decline. It may be a decline from a sideways market but most often it is seen when a rising market reverses direction. It is a definite change from an uptrend to a downtrend, lasting several weeks or longer.

breakaway gap: A gap that initiates a new trend. *See* gap.

breakeven: The point where there is neither profit or loss. For example, the market price needed to cover purchase price of a stock plus any commissions or fees.

breakout: Term used when a stock's price or volume moves significantly above or below its previously recorded resistance or support level. Generally, a new trend will be established and the price will continue in that direction.

break point: Share increments that will allow a reduction in commissions charged for the purchase of certain mutual funds.

broker: (1) One who acts as an agent for his or her clients. Brokers transact business on behalf of their clients and receive a commission for their service. Dealers, on the other hand, buy and sell for their own account. *Compare* dealer. (2) Common term for account executive or registered representative.

brokerage account: A formal record of all securities transactions ever handled for a client, a listing of all current holdings, and the current debit or credit balance.

brokerage house: Any firm acting as a broker or dealer in securities transactions. *Also called* brokerage firm.

broker-dealer: A firm that acts as both a.broker and a dealer. The firm may act as an agent for its clients, charging a commission for its services, or act as a dealer, buying and selling for its own account and charging its clients a markup or markdown. The firm must indicate in which capacity it has acted for each transaction.

broker's loan: Money borrowed from banks by security brokers and dealers to finance underwritings, cover purchases in customers' margin accounts, or finance inventories of securities.

bucket shop: An illegal brokerage operation in which an operator accepts a security order and money from a client but does not execute the security order, or executes it, but in a manner favorable to the operation rather than the client.

bull: One who believes a market and the economy in general will be favorable and rise. *Compare* bear.

bullion: Gold or silver that has been refined and presented in the form of bars or ingots.

bullish: Positive sentiment regarding a market or the economy in general with the expectation that market prices will rise. *Compare* bearish.

bull market: A market in which the general trend of security prices is up for a long period of time, several months or more. *Compare* bear market.

bull spread: A spread option strategy in which the investor buys one type of option (either a call or put) and sells the other on the same underlying stock simultaneously. The option that is sold will have a higher striking (exercise) price than the one that is purchased. The investor expects to profit by an increase in the market price of the underlying security. *Compare* bear spread.

bull straddle writing: Option writing (selling) strategy involving an uncovered put option and a covered call option on the same underlying security. *Compare* bear straddle writing.

business cycle: Broad repeated periodic fluctuations of economic activity.

business risk: The risk related to the prospects for a new business to obtain success. Some factors determining business risk include management ability, competition, development of new products, and price of goods.

bust: A period of major economic decline accompanied by falling stock prices, falling profits, and increasing unemployment.

butterfly spread: A spread option strategy involving the sale of two options and the purchase of two options for which the striking prices are of equal distance from the other in a ratio of 1:2:1. *Also called* sandwich spread.

buy a call: The investor pays a premium for a stock option contract that gives him the right to purchase 100 shares of a particular security at a specified price within a certain period of time.

buy a put: The investor pays a premium for a stock option contract that gives him the right to sell 100 shares of a particular security at a specified price within a certain period of time.

buyer: The option client who has purchased a contract that gives the right to either buy the underlying security in the case of a call, or sell the security in the case of a put, at a predetermined price within a specified period of time. *Also called* holder.

buyer's market: A market in which supply exceeds demand.

buyer's option: Security transaction in which the buyer determines the delivery date for the securities involved. If the seller delivers the securities before that date, the buyer has the option to reject them. *Compare* seller's option trade.

buy-in: Closing out a position in a client's account where securities have been sold, by repurchasing those securities. Buy-ins occur when the wrong security has been sold or when the client fails to deliver the securities he has sold.

buying power: The current amount of credit available in a margin account for purchasing additional securities. It is the dollar value of marginable securities a brokerage client may purchase or sell short in his margin account without adding additional money or securities. (SMA in an account may be used to purchase nonmarginable securities.) *See* margin, special miscellaneous account.

buying range: A price range in a declining market determined by analysts to be a probable turnaround area and therefore a recommended time to make an investment.

buy-limit order: *See* limit order.

buy order: Verbal or written authorization given by an investor to a broker or dealer to puchase a stated number of shares of a specific security at market price or a limit price including any other trading instructions. *See* order. *Compare* sell order.

buy signal: Technical indicators indicate that a stock is in a pattern that will soon lead to an up-reversal. *Compare* sell signal.

cabinet bid: An off-the-floor transaction to close an out-of-the-money (worthless) options contract at $1.00 per contract.

calculated risk: Estimated probability of success; the unknowns associated with an investment or venture but judged to be worth undertaking.

calendar spread: A spread option strategy in which the investor simultaneously purchases and sells options (either puts or call) on the same underlying stock with same strike (exercise) price but with different expiration dates. *Also called* horizontal spread, time spread.

calendar bear spread: *See* horizontal bear spread.

calendar bull spread: *See* horizontal bull spread.

call: An option contract which gives the holder (buyer) the right to purchase 100 shares of a specific stock at a stated price within a given period of time. Compare put.

callable bond: A bond permitting the issuer to call-in and redeem the bond before maturity date. Terms allowing this must be stated in the indenture at the time of issue. Face value plus a premium is normally paid to the bondholder if a bond is called-in prior to maturity.

callable preferred stock: Preferred stock that allows the issuer to call-in and redeem the stock. Terms allowing this must be stated at the time of issuance.

call away: The right of a call option holder (buyer) to purchase, in 100-share lots, a particular security at a specific price from the seller who has written an option contract on those shares.

call date: The date on which a bond issue or preferred stock may be redeemed in whole or part prior to maturity as stipulated at the time of issuance.

called: *See* exercised, redeem.

call loan: Loan in which there is no set maturity date. Either party may terminate the loan, the lender by calling-in the loan or the borrower by paying off the loan. Loans made by banks to security brokers and dealers are of this type.

call money market: Market in which brokers and dealers borrow money to meet credit needs. *Also called* New York call money.

call option buy/sell ratio: Call option buying divided by call option selling. A higher ratio during a downtrend usually indicates a bearish sentiment and a lower ratio during an uptrend usually indicates a bullish sentiment.

call price: The total of face value plus any premium at which an issuer will redeem a callable security.

call protection: Provision in the terms of issuance of a callable security which gives protection to the holder that the security may not be called-in and redeemed before a certain time period has passed.

call spread: An option spread position created by purchasing a call on a particular security and writing a call with a different expiration date, different exercise price, or both on the same security.

capital: (1) Paid in capital. The amount invested in a business by its owners or shareholders. (2) Net worth. The amount invested by owners or shareholders plus retained earnings. (3) The wealth of an individual used to obtain greater affluence.

capital asset: The fixed, relatively permanent assets of a corporation including land, buildings, machinery, and so on.

capital gains: (1) Profit received from the sale of an asset, such as securities or real estate. (2) Long-term capital gains are those which have been held long enough to receive special tax considerations. (3) Short-term capital gains are those for which the profits are taxed as ordinary income.

capital gains distribution: Distributions made by mutual funds to shareholders that represent a pro rata share of the net capital gains realized by the sale of securities within the fund.

capital intense industry: An industry that requires a large degree of capital investment in relation to the total of individuals working in that industry. *Compare* labor intense industry.

capitalism: An economic system in which ownership and investment for profit by private individuals is encouraged.

capitalization: The longer-term or relatively permanent funds used to finance a business operation such as bonds, preferred stock, and common stock.

capital loss: (1) Loss incurred on the sale of an asset such as securities or real estate. (2) Long-term capital losses are those that have been held long enough to receive special tax treatment. (3) Short-term capital losses are those that may be deducted against ordinary income.

capital markets: Financial securities markets that trade instruments that are long-term or forms of permanent capitalization. This would include bonds, common stock, and preferred stock. *Compare* money markets.

capital risk: The risk that an investor may not recover all or a portion of his original capital at the time an investment is liquidated. For example, this can occur when fixed income investments are liquidated prior to maturity during a period of relatively higher interest rates.

capital stock: All classes and types of stock issued by a corporation that represent ownership. However, this term is usually used in reference to common stock.

capping: Manipulative and illegal practice where persons attempt to keep the market price of an underlying security from trading above a certain exercise price of a stock option contract.

carat: A unit of weight for precious stones. *Compare* karat.

cash account: A brokerage account in which purchases and sales of securities must be concluded no later than the settlement date. No credit or margin is extended.

cash dividend: A dividend paid out in the form of money rather than additional shares of stock, bonds, or other types of property. This is the most commonly issued form of dividends.

cash equivalent: (1) The value of an asset if immediately exchanged for cash. (2) In accounting, any item that may be easily converted to cash with little or no change in current market value, such as securities, notes, and so on.

cash management bills: Short-term money market instruments issued by the U.S. Treasury to fund very short-term financial needs.

cash trades: A security order that is executed for immediate delivery. Settlement must take place at the time the transaction is made.

CBOE: *See* Chicago Board Options Exchange.

CD: *See* certificate of deposit.

certificateless trading: A system for transacting the purchase and sale of securities in which no certificates of ownership are issued to the holder (buyer) of a security. Evidence of ownership may usually be obtained, upon request of the holder, in the form of a non-negotiable certificate issued in the name of the broker who originally executed the transaction.

certificate of deposit: (1) Negotiable money market instrument issued by banks for $100,000 or more for 30 days or more that have negotiated rates. These trade on the open market and offer the investor an excellent return

and high degree of safety. (2) Non-negotiable instrument issued by banks to individuals. These offer an excellent return and high degree of safety but are not negotiable and carry high penalties for early withdrawal.

charting: A graphic method of depicting stock prices and other data that might influence prices. Chartists believe that analysis of past and present patterns can be used to predict future price direction. Several types of charts are in use, each with its own distinct advantages and disadvantages. The three basic types are line charts, bar charts, and point-and-figure charts.

chartist: One who studies and interprets chart signals and patterns, averages and indicators, and other technical information to predict future price movements.

Chicago Board of Trade: The largest commodity exchange in the United States. Address: 141 West Jackson Boulevard, Chicago, Illinois 60604.

Chicago Board Options Exchange: The first organized exchange in the United States to trade in stock option contracts. Address: 141 West Jackson Blvd., Chicago, Illinois 60604.

Chicago Mercantile Exchange: 444 West Jackson Boulevard, Chicago, Illinois 60606.

churning: Unethical practice of creating unnecessary transactions in an account in order to generate commissions without regard for the net effect on the client.

Cincinnati Stock Exchange: address: 205 Dixie Terminal Building, Cincinnati, Ohio 45202.

class of options: All option contracts of the same type on the same underlying security. For example, all call options on the ABC Corporation are of the same class.

clearing house: A facility used to execute and settle transactions between member firms. *Also called* clearing corporation.

clearing member: A member of an exchange who has been admitted to membership in a clearing corporation.

Clifford trust: A temporary trust in which all income generated during the life of the trust belongs to the person(s) for whom the trust was established. The trust must be established for a minimum of ten years. After the trust has ended, all assets revert back to the person who established the trust.

climax: A trading period of very heavy volume following a long-term rise or decline in market prices. This is then followed by relatively little continued increase or decrease in price, signaling a top or bottom.

close: (1) The end of trading for a security or exchange for a particular trading day. (2) The closing price of a security or exchange or index average. (3) To effect a closing option transaction. To terminate/eliminate an open option position. *See* closing transaction. *Compare* opening transaction.

closed account: A brokerage account that has been terminated by either the client or by the brokerage house. Past records are kept on file, but all securities and money are sent to the client or his representative.

closed corporation: A corporation in which ownership shares and voting control are held by a relatively limited number of individuals with the remaining shares being held by the public. *Also called* a closely held corporation.

closed-end investment company: Investment company that issues only one offering of shares to the public. The shares then trade on the open market and are not redeemable upon demand as in mutual funds. *See* investment company. *Compare* mutual fund, open-end investment company.

closed-end mortgage bond: Bond issue that stipulates that the property that

secures this bond may not be repledged as collateral on subsequent bond issues.

close-to-the-money: An option contract, either put or call, for which the striking price is very near the current market value of the underlying security.

closing price: The last trading price of any security for a particular trading day.

closing purchase transaction: A stock option transaction in which the writer of an option contract reduces or liquidates his position and ends his obligation to buy or sell shares of the underlying security upon which those contracts were written. *Compare* opening sale transaction.

closing rotation: *See* trading rotation.

closing sale transaction: A stock option transaction in which the holder of an option contract reduces or liquidates his position and ends his right to buy or sell shares of the underlying security upon which those contracts were based. *Compare* opening purchase transaction.

closing transaction: The purchase or sale of an option contract that terminates an open position and ends all rights or obligations to buy or sell shares on the underlying security. *Compare* opening transaction.

coincident indicators: Economic indicators that move at approximately the same time and same direction that the general economy is moving. Some coincident indicators commonly followed are personal income, employment, and gross national product. *Compare* leading indicators, lagging indicators.

collateral: Securities or other property used to secure a loan.

collateral trust bond: A bond secured by collateral that has been placed on deposit with a trustee in accordance with terms of the bond issuance. Stocks and bonds of other companies are often used as collateral. *Also called* collateral trust certificate.

combination: A stock-option position that is similar to a straddle, involving a put and a call on the same underlying security but having different striking prices.

COMEX: *See* Commodity Exchange of New York.

commercial paper: Short-term negotiable money market instruments issued by major corporations to secure short-term funds. Commercial paper is typically issued at a discount and trades on the open market.

commission: Fee charged by a broker, agent, or other intermediary as remuneration for services.

commission house broker: *See* floor broker.

Committee on Uniform Securities Identification Procedures (CUSIP): Committee set up by the American Bankers Association to set standards for identifying securities. Every common and preferred stock and every corporate and municipal bond is assigned its own CUSIP number.

Commodity Exchange of New York (COMEX): Address: 4 World Trade Center, New York, New York 10048.

commodity futures: *See* futures.

Commodity Futures Trading Commission: The commission that regulates trading on the commodity exchanges. Address: 2033 K Street N.W., Washington, D.C. 20581.

common stock: Shares representing individual ownership in a corporation. These shares are not limited in nor do they receive preference in the distribution of any corporate earnings. This class of stock represents ownership of the corporation after all liabilities and other claims have been taken into account.

common stock fund: A type of mutual fund that invests primarily in common stocks for greater growth of capital.

compliance registered options principal (CROP): The person charged with the audit responsibility to determine that a brokerage firm's option activities are conducted in compliance with current laws, SEC regulations, and SRO rules.

competitive bid underwriting: Bidding among several underwriters for the right to handle all or part of a new issue. Offering price is determined by the bidding process.

composites: Averages using data from several sources to measure results. The Dow Jones Composite uses data from the industrial, transportation, and utility averages.

concession: The amount by which a security's market price will increase when a block of that stock is bought, or reduced when a block is sold.

confidence index: *See* Barron's Confidence Index.

confirmation: In market analysis, confirmation indicates that two or more indexes or averages confirm a trend or turning point in the market.

confirmation slip: The acknowledgement sent to a client by the brokerage firm which verifies the transaction made on the client's behalf. It normally includes the name of the security, number of shares traded, whether bought or sold, price per share, commissions and fees, and the net dollar amount of the transaction. *Also called* transaction slip.

conglomerate: Corporation operating in a number of more or less unrelated business areas.

conservative portfolio: A portfolio designed with safety of capital as its primary objective. It may include stocks and/or bonds, but each investment is prudently chosen for its safety.

Consolidated Tape: This reports transactions of both national exchanges and may report transactions on some or all regional exchanges and over-the-counter transactions. *Also called* Unified Tape.

Consolidated Tape Association: The organization that developed and operates the Consolidated Tape System.

consolidation: (1) A short-term pause in the direction of a stock's movement with the expectation that the established price direction will resume. (2) Combining two or more separate organizations into one new corporation.

constant ratio plan: One of several formula investing plans. The plan calls for keeping a certain dollar ratio in two types of investments. For example, if investment capital starts at $25,000 and the plan calls for a 50/50 ratio in stocks and bonds, $12,500 would be committed to each. If the value of the stocks then rose to $20,000 and the bonds remained steady, an adjustment would be made to return to the 50/50 ratio.

Consumer Price Index: Index issued monthly by the Bureau of Labor Statistics that relates changes in the prices of basic consumer goods and services, including food, housing, fuel, medical care, and so on.

continued bond: A bond that bears no definite maturity date and may continue to pay interest indefinitely. *Also called* annuity bond.

contract: An agreement between two or more persons creating mutual obligations.

contractual plan: A plan available with some mutual funds for the purchase of additional fund shares. The investor agrees to purchase a fixed dollar amount on an installment basis. Cancellation is allowed, but most sales charges must be paid in the early years of the contract.

control person: Any individual who can influence the management actions or policies of a corporation. This includes directors, officers, and shareholders owning 10 percent or more of shares outstanding.

conversion: (1) Switching from one mutual fund to another fund that is controlled by the same management and in the same family of funds. (2) Exchanging one type of security for another. Convertible bonds and convertible preferred stock have conversion privileges. (3) The unlawful taking of something of value that belongs to someone else. (4) Technique used in option trading that involves changing one side of an option straddle contract into the other side of the straddle. As market changes occur in the underlying security, one may convert puts to calls or calls to puts.

conversion charge: (1) A fee charged by some mutual funds to switch from one fund to another that is operated by the same management and in the same family of mutual funds. (2) A charge for converting one side of a straddle option position into the other side.

conversion parity: The point of equality in conversion. The current market value of common stock being equal to the conversion privilege of the convertible issue.

conversion price: The price at which conversion of one security into another may be made.

conversion ratio: The number of shares of stock or the number of bonds that are required to convert from a convertible security into the underlying security. This ratio is determined at the time the convertible security is issued.

convertible bond: A debt instrument issued with the privilege of conversion for a specified number of shares of the common stock or another security of the same issuer at a specific price.

convertible preferred stock: Shares of preferred stock issued with the privilege of conversion for a specific number of shares of the common stock of the same issuer at a specific price.

corner: Controlling sufficient shares of stock to affect the supply and the market price of that security.

corporation: A legal entity operating under a state charter or articles of incorporation, owned by an unlimited number of individuals. In the majority of corporations, the owner's or shareholder's liability is limited to his interest in the corporation.

corporate bond: A debt security issued by public corporations and backed by either specific assets of the corporation or the credit-worthiness of the corporation. Corporate bonds normally have a stated life and pay a fixed rate of interest semiannually. Corporate bonds do not represent ownership in the corporation. The principal classes of corporate bonds are mortgage bonds, collateral trust bonds, equipment trust certificates, guaranteed bonds, and debentures.

corporate charter: The legal document, state-approved certified articles of incorporation, that states the name of the corporation, its location, amount and form of capitalization, intended activities, the types of securities to be issued, and the uses of funds received.

corporate reacquisition: The attempt of a corporation to repurchase its own securities through a tender offer.

correspondent bank: A bank that has a direct relationship with another bank and performs services for the other.

correspondent firm: A brokerage firm that has a direct relationship with another brokerage firm and performs services for the other.

cost basis: Value of assets. Original cost minus any depreciation or the fair market value at the time of purchase.

cost-push inflation: Inflation caused by increasing costs of labor and materials which result in an increase in the price of goods.

counter-cyclical securities: Securities issued by corporations whose earnings generally fluctuate in the opposite direction of the general economic trend.

coupon: The certificate attached to a bond that is cut off and presented for interest payment. Each coupon is dated and shows the amount of interest due.

coupon bond: A bearer bond with coupons attached that must be clipped and presented to a disbursing agent for interest payment.

coupon rate: Interest rate stated for any bond. The rate is quoted as an annual percentage rate of face value.

coupon yield: Yield calculated by dividing the annual interest payment by the face value of a bond. Coupon yield is equivalent to coupon rate.

cover: To purchase or present shares of a security to replace those shares that have been sold short.

coverage ratio: Relationship between debt interest payments and pretax income. These ratios are used to determine the ability of a corporation to cover its debt service.

covered: A short position that is hedged by a long position in the same underlying security or its equivalent.

covered call: A short call option position that is protected by either a long position in the underlying security or its equivalent, or by a long call option for an equivalent number of shares for which the exercise price is equal to or less than the exercise price of the call that was written.

covered call writer: The writer (seller) of a call stock option contract who holds a hedged position in the underlying security.

covered option writing: Option strategy involving the sale of option contracts that are hedged by long option positions or by shares of the underlying security.

covered put: A short put position that is protected by a long put option for an equivalent number of shares for which the exercise price is equal to or greater than the exercise price of the put that was written.

covered put writer: The writer (seller) of a put stock option contract who holds a hedged position in the underlying security.

crash: A depression. Sudden and severe decline in the economy and securities markets.

credit: A bookkeeping entry on the right side of an account that results from the reduction or elimination of an asset or expense, or the creation or addition to a liability or revenue.

credit balance: In a brokerage account, a credit balance is the money balance in the account that belongs to the investor and that may be used to make additional investments.

credit risk: Risk that the issuer of a debt instrument will default either on interest payments or principal payment or both.

credit spread: A spread option position for which the price of the long option is less than the price of the short option—therefore creating a credit in the brokerage account. *Compare* debit spread.

CROP: *See* compliance registered options principal.

crossing: Off-the-floor matching of a transaction involving a large number of shares between two parties. This is done to maintain an orderly market and maintain price balance.

crowd: *See* trading crowd.

cum dividend: With dividend. Buyer of a stock trading cum dividend will receive the dividend that has been

declared but not yet paid. *Compare* ex-dividend.

cum rights: With rights. Buyer of a stock trading cum rights will receive the rights that have been declared but not yet paid. *Compare* ex-rights.

cumulative dividend: Dividend due on cumulative preferred stock that is in arrears.

cumulative preferred stock: A type of preferred stock issued with the stipulation that any and all dividends that are not paid will accumulate for the benefit of the holders before any dividends may be paid to common shareholders.

cumulative voting: Shareholders' voting privilege that allows one vote for each share of stock times the number of seats on the board of directors to be filled. For example, in voting for five directors, a shareholder with 200 shares would have a total of 1,000 votes that he could cast for one director or in any other manner he chooses. *Compare* statutory voting.

Curb Exchange: Original name of the American Stock Exchange.

current assets: Cash and other liquid assets that can easily be converted into cash. Those assets that will be turned into income within a year or less.

current liabilities: Short-term debts that are due and payable in one year or less.

current market value: The value of securities in an account based on the closing price of the previous trading day.

current ratio: Calculated by dividing current assets by current liabilities. This ratio is used to measure the short-term financial strength of a company.

current yield: The annual dividend or interest paid on a security stated as a percentage of current market price (not acquisition price).

35

CUSIP: *See* Committee on Uniform Securities Identification Procedures.

CUSIP number: Number assigned to every common stock, preferred stock, corporate bond, and municipal bond for security identification purposes.

custodian: An individual who is responsible for the activities in the brokerage account of another person. For example, the custodian of a minor's account.

customer agreement: *See* margin agreement.

customer's broker: Preferred terms are registered representative or account executive.

cycle: (1) One completed interval of up and down economic or market movements. Cycles may vary in duration and volatility. (2) The months in which stock option contracts expire. *See* expiration cycle.

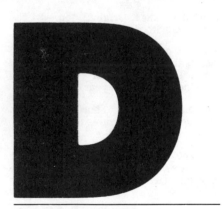

daily high: The highest price reached by a security or market average during a specific trading day. This is not necessarily the opening or closing price.

daily low: The lowest price reached by a security or market average during a specific trading day. This is not necessarily the opening or closing price.

dated date: Date assigned by underwriters as the effective date of a new issue. Normally, the dated date is the same as the issue date.

dated earned surplus: Retained earnings of a corporation that have accumulated from the date of a reorganization. On the balance sheet, the reorganization date must be included when reporting retained earnings.

day loans: Loans made to brokers and dealers by financial institutions to supply working capital for that day only.

day order: An order given by an investor to buy or sell a specific number of shares of a particular security at market or a limit price on the day the order is placed or it is automatically canceled at the end of that trading date. *See* order. *Compare* good until canceled order.

day trading: Buying securities and selling them the same day; or shorting stock and covering the short position on the same day to take advantage of intraday price fluctuations.

dealer: One who buys for his or her own account and then resells from that inventory. The dealer differs from the broker in that a broker merely represents the buyer or seller. Over-the-counter transactions are usually handled by dealers. Most brokerage firms may act as either broker or dealer depending on the transaction, but they must indicate in which capacity they have acted. *Also called* principal. *Compare* broker.

Dealer Bank Association: Address: 1800 K Street N.W., Suite 1014, Washington D.C. 20006.

debenture: An unsecured longer-term debt obligation backed only by the general credit of the issuing corporation.

debenture bond: An unsecured long-term instrument backed only by the general credit of the issuer. The bond indenture may stipulate certain safety measures to protect the bondholders.

debit: A bookkeeping entry on the left side of an account that results from the creation of or addition to an asset or expense or the elimination or reduction of a liability revenue. *Compare* credit.

debit balance: In a brokerage account, a debit balance is the money owed to the brokerage firm for security transactions plus any interest and fees that have not been paid by the investor.

debit spread: A spread option position for which the price of the long option is greater than the price of the short option—therefore creating a debit in the brokerage account. *Compare* credit spread.

debt: Goods, money, or services owed by one to another.

debt/equity ratio: Calculated by dividing long-term debt by stockholder's equity, this ratio is used to measure the risk associated with the capital structure of a corporation.

debt financing: Issuing notes or bonds to raise capital to meet financial needs in contrast to equity financing where shares of stock are issued. *Compare* equity financing.

debt limit: The maximum debt that any governmental unit may legally incur.

debt security: Bonds or notes issued by a corporation or government unit to raise capital. Debt securities normally have a stated life and pay a fixed rate of interest. *Compare* equity security.

declaration date: The date on which the corporation announces that a dividend will be paid, stating the record date, payment date, and the amount of the dividend. *Also called* announcement date.

deep discount bonds: Bonds selling substantially below face value; a general measure is below $800 on a bond with a face value of $1,000.

deep-in-the-money: (1) A call option contract for which the striking (exercise) price is substantially below the market price of the underlying security. (2) A put option contract for which the striking (exercise) price is substantially above the market price of the underlying security.

default: (1) Failure to perform any contractual obligation. (2) Failure to pay interest and/or principal on a bond or note on payment date.

defensive industry: An industry that is not as adversely affected by poor economic conditions as other industries or the general economy. Securities of these firms usually perform better than the market as a whole during economic slumps or recessions because these companies are able to maintain relatively good earnings. One example is the utilities industry.

defensive investing: A portfolio designed to lessen risk and vulnerability during periods of market and economic declines. The primary objectives are safety of principal, income, and stability of market price.

defensive issues: Securities that remain relatively stable even in periods of economic slumps. Some defensive issues include high grade corporate bonds, government and municipal bonds, certificates of deposit, commercial paper, and utility stocks.

deflation: Period in which the purchasing power of the dollar increases. Periods of deflation are usually accompanied by a drop in wages, higher unemployment, and lower costs for goods and services. *Compare* inflation.

delayed delivery: Settlement of a security transaction in which physical delivery of the certificates or payment of money will be delayed beyond the normal settlement date. Delayed delivery must be approved by all parties involved in the transaction.

delayed opening: The temporary delaying of the opening of trading of a particular security. This is done in order to maintain a fair and orderly market due to a large influx of buy or sell orders or due to some major announcement. The specialist must obtain exchange approval to delay an opening.

delist: Exchange action of removing a security's right to be traded on the floor of that exchange. Usually the reason for this action is because the company no longer meets the minimum exchange requirements. The securities will then usually be traded in the over-the-counter market.

delivery: Completion of security transaction by physical delivery of the certificates and payment of funds within the settlement period. *See* good delivery.

delivery vs. payment (DVP): A securities transaction with the provision that payment will be made upon delivery of the securities. The certificates are delivered to a bank designated by the investor; the bank will then make payment upon receipt of the certificates.

demand: The total desire for an economic good or service. *Compare* supply.

demand deposit: Deposits in financial institutions that may be claimed by depositors without advance notice to the institution and with no penalty to the depositor.

demand note: Short-term financial obligation that does not have a stated maturity date and may be called-in for payment at any time.

demand-pull inflation: Inflation resulting from conditions where demand exceeds supply. Prices will rise due to greater demand which in turn will result in a demand for higher wages resulting in higher cost for goods and services. Money supply and available credit will also increase for a period of time. *Compare* cost-push inflation.

demographic trends: Analytical tool used to project population trends and their affect on particular industries and economic needs.

depletion: (1) Periodic reduction in the value of a resource allowed for tax and accounting purposes due to the decreasing quantity of the resource (such as timber, oil, and natural gas). (2) The exhaustion in the supply of a resource. *Compare* depreciation.

Depository Trust Company: A centralized depository for security certificates through which delivery of securities between member firms takes place via computerized entries.

depreciation: (1) Periodic reduction in the value of an asset allowed for tax and accounting purposes due to the loss of usefulness of the asset. (2) The wasting away of an asset due to wear and tear or obsolescence. *Compare* depletion.

depressed price: Market price for a security that is lower than justified considering the fundamental conditions of the company.

depression: State of long severe economic decline, more serious than a recession, in which there is a high rate of unemployment, a large number of business failures, and declining market prices.

Designated Order Turnaround System (DOT): The NYSE electronic system for handling orders, which allows member firms to place day market and limit orders. Through this system the specialist receives the order, presents it to the trading crowd for execution, and a confirmation of the execution is sent back to the firm placing the order.

devaluation: Action by a government to lower the value of its currency in relation to currencies of other countries.

diagonal spread: An option strategy involving the simultaneous sale of options of the same class on the same underlying security but with different striking (exercise) prices and different expiration dates.

differential: Charge made by most brokerage houses for handling odd-lot transactions. This differential is usually 1/8 of a point.

dilution: Reducing equity ratio, earnings per share, and book value per share as represented by a single ownership share. This is caused by the issuance of additional shares of stock without a corresponding increase in income or assets.

direct placement: *See* private placement.

director: An individual elected by the stockholders at the annual meeting to represent the shareholders in establishing company policies. *See* board of directors.

disbursement: The payment of funds, such as dividends.

disbursing agent: Person or institution that handles the payment of dividends or interest to shareholders.

disclosure: Revealing all pertinent facts regarding the management, financial status, and any legal matters surrounding a corporation. Disclosure is required in all securities offerings. *See* full disclosure.

discount: (1) The amount by which the current market price is below face or par value. *Compare* premium. (2) A reduction or allowance in price. (3) A method of charging interest in which the total interest due is subtracted from the proceeds of the loan at the time the loan is made. U.S. Treasury bills are issued in this manner. (4) To evaluate and anticipate future trends and estimate the present value of those trends. Market prices tend to anticipate future corporate and economic conditions.

discount bond: Bond for which the current market value is below face value. For example, a $1,000 face value bond selling for $900. The investor would receive interest each year that the bond is held plus $1,000 at maturity.

discount brokerage firm: Securities broker who offers substantially lower commission rates on security transactions than full-service brokerage firms. In 1975, the Securities and Exchange Commission ruled that fixed pricing for securities transactions would be eliminated, giving rise to the development of the discount brokerage industry. The discount brokerage industry is able to offer fast executions and low commission rates by eliminating some of the services that are not used by all investors, such as investment research.

discounting the news: Investors' tendency to evaluate and anticipate future expectations for a corporation and the economy, estimate the present value of those trends, and act accordingly before the events actually occur. For example, if an economic recovery is expected in the near future, market prices will tend to move up several months before the start of the recovery.

discount rate: The rate of interest set by the Federal Reserve that member banks are charged when borrowing money through the Federal Reserve System.

discretionary account: A brokerage account in which the client gives partial or full authority in writing to a broker or other advisor to transact securities business at his or her discretion. This may include what to buy/sell, when to buy/sell and at what price.

discretionary income: Income that is left after meeting all essential expenses to maintain one's current standard of living. This income is then available for savings, investments, leisure, and travel.

discretionary order: A verbal or written authorization from a client that has been approved by the broker or advisor to handle a single security transaction at his or her discretion. This authorization is for one transaction only.

disintermediation: Withdrawal of funds (i.e. savings accounts) previously invested with financial institutions who have governmental imposed limits as to the interest they pay and who act as portfolio intermediaries, and then investing those funds in higher yield securities, such as corporate bonds. *Compare* intermediation.

disposable income: All income an individual receives after meeting tax obligations. This includes money to meet essential living expenses, funds for emergencies, and discretionary income.

distribution: (1) Distributing a security to the public through a primary offering or disposing of a large block of stock through a secondary offering. (2) The demand for a stock is less than the expanding supply of that stock. This will usually have an unfavorable effect on the price. Distribution generally occurs during a neutral price trend where supply gradually exceeds demand. *Compare* accumulation. (3) Distributing cash or stock dividends to shareholders. (4) Distributing dividends or capital gains to shareholders of mutual funds.

distribution date: The date on which a dividend or other payment or distribution is made to holders of an instrument. *Also called* payment date.

divergence: (1) A period in which the prevailing trend of a market average or a security is not in line with technical indicators. This usually suggests that a change in the trend will occur. (2) In technical analysis, two or more indexes or averages that do not show confirming patterns.

diversification: Distribution of risk in a portfolio by investing in several types of investments or several different corporations.

divest: To dispose of an investment or asset. For example, a corporation selling a subsidiary.

divided account: A syndication method in which each member of the underwriting syndicate is responsible only for its own allocation and not for any other member. *Also called* Western account. *Compare* Eastern account, undivided account.

dividend: Payment by a corporation to its shareholders which represents earnings of the company. Payment is made on a pro rata basis. A dividend is typi-cally quoted on a per share annual payment basis. The dividend may be in the form of cash, additional shares of stock or other property.

dividend payout ratio: Dividends per share on common stock divided by earnings per share.

dividend reinvestment plan: (1) A program offered by mutual funds that allows shareholders to have their dividends automatically reinvested in additional shares of the corporation.

DJIA: *See* Dow Jones Industrial Average.

DK: *See* don't know order.

DNR: *See* do not reduce order.

dollar bonds: Municipal bonds that trade on a dollar basis rather than on a yield to maturity basis.

dollar cost averaging: One of several formula investing plans that involves buying a fixed dollar amount of securities at regular intervals, for example $500 quarterly. When prices are high, fewer shares are purchased and when prices are lower more shares would be purchased.

domestic corporation: A corporation created under the laws of a certain state or country—when speaking of operations within that state or country. *Compare* foreign corporation.

donated capital stock: Shares of capital stock donated back to the issuing corporation by shareholders without any compensation.

do-not-reduce order (DNR): Trading instructions (qualifiers) given by an investor that prevent a sell-stop order, a sell-stop limit order, or a buy-limit order from being reduced by the amount of the ordinary cash dividend on ex-dividend date.

don't know order (DK): A designation on security transactions, delivery of securities, or payment of funds that indicates a refusal because the trade is unknown by that party.

dormant account: A brokerage account in which there has been no activity for an extended period of time. *See* inactive account.

DOT: *See* Designated Order Turnaround System.

double-barrelled bond: A municipal bond for which both interest and principal are secured by a revenue producing facility and by the full faith and credit of the issuing municipality.

double bottom: A "W"-shaped charted price formation that may occur after a period of declining prices and indicates a possible bottom to be followed by a period of advancing prices.

double digit inflation: A rate of inflation annually amounting to 10 percent or greater.

double taxation: Taxation of earnings of a corporation and then taxation to shareholders on dividends paid out of those after-tax corporate earnings.

double top: An "M" shaped charted price formation that may occur after a period of rising prices and indicates a possible peak to be followed by a period of declining prices.

Dow: Used in reference to the Dow Jones Averages but in particular to the Dow Jones Industrial Average.

Dow Jones Averages: Security price averages used as a representative indicator of general market prices.

Dow Jones Bond Average: Index computed using average prices from six different bond groups. This average is used to measure bond market strength.

Dow Jones Commodity Futures Index: An index calculated once every hour for twelve commodities taking into account the trading volume and production for each, as well as the unit trading prices and contract delivery dates.

Dow Jones Composite: A composite of the Dow Jones Industrial, Transportation, and Utility averages. *Also called* 65 Stock Average.

Dow Jones Industrial Average: Average computed from 30 leading blue-chip industrial stocks using an unweighted arithmetic mean and quoted in terms of points rather than dollars. It is used as a representative indicator of the movement of the markets in general but especially the New York Stock Exchange. The divisor for the average is adjusted for splits and dividends of 10 percent or greater to maintain comparability. At one time the divisor was 30; today it is under 1.50. The 30 stocks currently used in the Dow Jones Industrial Average are:
Allied Corp
Aluminum Co of America
American Brands
American Can
American Express
A T & T
Bethlehem Steel
DuPont
Eastman Kodak
Exxon
General Electric
General Foods
General Motors
Goodyear
Inco
IBM
Intl Harvester
Intl Paper
Merck
Minn. Mng & Mfg
Owens-Illinois
Procter & Gamble
Sears Roebuck
Standard Oil of Cal
Texaco
Union Carbide
United Technologies
U.S. Steel
Westinghouse
Woolworth

Dow Jones Municipal Index: Average computed weekly using the market value of leading municipal bonds that are selling at a discounted price.

Dow Jones Transportation Average: Average computed from 20 companies involved in various modes of transportation. The average is calculated in much the same manner as the Dow

Industrial Average. The twenty stocks currently used in the Transportion Average are:
AMR Corp
Burlington Northern
Canadian Pacific
Carolina Freight
Consolidated Freight
CSX Corp
Delta Air Lines
Eastern Air Lines
Norfolk Southern
Northwest Air
Overnite Transport
Pan Am World Air
Rio Grande Indus
Santa Fe Indus
Southern Pacific
Transway Intl
Trans World Corp
UAL Inc
Union Pacific Corp
U. S. Air Group

Dow Jones Utility Average: Average computed using 15 utility stocks. The average is computed in much the same manner of the Dow Industrial Average. The fifteen stocks currently used in the Utility Average are:
American Elec Pwr
Cleveland Elec Ill
Columbia Gas Sys
Commonwealth Ed
Consolidated Ed
Consolidated Natl Gas
Detroit Edison
Houston Indus
Niagara Mohawk Pwr
Pacific Gas & Elec
Panhandle Eastern
Peoples Energy
Philadelphia Elec
Public Ser Elec & Gas
Southern Cal Ed

down market: a period when there is a declining trend in market prices.

down reversal: A sudden decline in prices following an advancing trend. The term is used only to explain a short-term decline.

downside breakeven: The price to which a security must decline before an investor begins to incur a loss. *Compare* upside breakeven.

downside risk: An estimate using technical analysis to determine the lowest future market value of a stock. This may be a near, intermediate, or long-term price appraisal.

downside trend: A period of prolonged declining prices which may last for several months in which small up reversals may occur.

downtick: A transaction that occurs at a price lower than the previous transaction. For example, if XYZ sold at 25 then at 24 1/2, the second transaction is considered a downtick. *Compare* uptick.

down trend: A security's prevailing price direction is declining.

Dow theory: Analytical theory based on present movements of the Dow Jones Industrial Average and the Dow Jones Transportation Average. The theory states that if either of these averages moves above an important previous high and is followed by a move in the other index, the market in general is moving upward. When both averages fall below an important previous low it is considered a confirmation that the market in general is in a down trend.

dual listing: The listing of a single security on more than one exchange. For example, a security may be listed both on the American Exchange and the Pacific Exchange.

dual-purpose fund: A closed-end investment company that issues two classes of stock. One class is considered income shares and receives all interest and dividends that are accumulated. The other class is entitled to all capital gains distributions that are realized from capital growth.

due bill: An acknowledgment that the issuer will forward to the holder something that is due him. For example, if shares are sold after the record date on a stock split, but before issuance date, the sale must be accompanied by a due bill acknowledging that the seller must deliver the additional shares sold to the buyer.

due date: (1) Date on which the principal payment must be made on a debt obligation. (2) Settlement date for a security transaction.

due diligence: Investigation by representatives of an underwriting syndicate to determine that all material information about a pending new issue is released to the public.

duplicate confirmation: A copy of a confirmation slip that is sent to another person, in addition to the one that is sent to the client.

earned growth rate: The compounded annual internal rate at which a corporation's equity per share grows as a result of reinvestment of earnings.

earned surplus: Retained earnings. The net earnings of a company that are not paid out in the form of dividends but rather retained in the business.

earning power: Valuation of estimated earnings of an asset or security and the present value of those estimated earnings.

earnings: Net profit after all expenses and taxes have been paid, but before dividends are paid out to shareholders.

earnings multiple: *See* price/earnings ratio.

earnings per share: Net profit less preferred stock obligations divided by the number of shares of common stock outstanding.

earnings report: Commonly called profit and loss statement or income statement. The earnings report presents all income, expenses, and the net profit or loss for a business.

Eastern account: Common syndication method used in underwriting municipal securities. Each member of the syndication has undivided liability in underwriting and selling the issue. *Also called* undivided account. *Compare* Western account.

easy money: A period in which the money supply is expanding and there is a relatively ready supply of lendable money.

economic activity: The production and distribution of goods and services.

economic analysis: The study and interpretation of the fundamental conditions of the economy and forecasting future economic trends.

economic indicators: Factors that attempt to measure the nation's economic activity and attempt to forecast future activity. These include employment, wages, prices, and other factors.

either/or order: Trading instructions given by an investor to the broker to have an order executed in either of two alternatives. When execution of one alternative takes place, the other is cancelled. *See* alternative order.

eligible list: Similar to approved list or legal list. A list of securities that financial institutions may purchase as investments. These lists are prepared by representatives of financial institutions.

eligible paper: Various notes, banker's acceptances, and commercial paper that banks, which are members of the Federal Reserve System, may submit for rediscounting.

Employee Retirement Income Security Act (ERISA): A federal act governing the administration and management of pension fund money and requiring those involved to act as fiduciaries and follow the prudent man rule when making investment decisions and requiring proper disclosure to the Department of Labor and the Internal Revenue Service.

Employee Stock Ownership Plan: Corporate program available in some companies that allows employees to invest in shares of the firm for which they are employed through contribution plans.

endorsed bond: A bond that is guaranteed by a corporation other than the issuing corporation. *Also called* guaranteed bond.

energy issues: Securities of corporations engaged in finding, developing, or producing energy products and those in energy-related fields.

energy trends: Analytical tool used to project main sources of fuel for energy production and their affect on particular industries and the economy.

enterprise: A business venture or organization.

EPS: *See* earnings per share.

equipment trust certificates: Debt instruments issued by companies for purchasing rolling stock equipment, such as rail cars. The equipment serves as collateral for the debt. *See* New York plan and Philadelphia plan.

equity: (1) The net worth of a corporation. (2) Dollars invested into a corporation as represented by shares of stock. (3) Proportional ownership of a corporation by a shareholder. (4) That portion which is paid up on an installment purchase plan.

equity capital: Capital received into a corporation through sale of shares of stock. Equity capital represents ownership, whereas bonds and notes represent debt.

equity financing: Selling equity shares to obtain capital for financing corporate needs. *Compare* debt financing.

equity security: Any security that represents ownership of a corporation. This includes not only common stock, but also preferred stock, rights, and warrants.

equivalent taxable yield: Yield comparison of tax-free interest income to after-tax income from another taxable invesment. Calculated by dividing tax-free yield by one (1) minus the investors' tax bracket. The chart below indicates what the investor would have to earn on a taxable invesment to achieve the same yield as on a tax free investment.

tax bracket	tax free yield			
	6.00%	8.00%	10.00%	12.00%
	equivalent taxable yield			
33.0	8.97	11.94	14.93	17.91
38.0	9.96	12.90	16.13	19.35
45.0	10.91	14.55	18.18	21.82
50.0	12.00	16.00	20.00	24.00

ERISA: *See* Employee Retirement Income Security Act.

escrow receipt: An acknowledgment provided by an approved depository that guarantees that securities or funds are on deposit at that bank and will be delivered upon an option contract being exercised.

estate: (1) Any right or interest in real or personal property. (2) The property, possessions, and interests of a deceased person.

estate tax: The federal and/or state tax imposed upon all or a portion of the estate of a deceased person.

estate tax bond: A long-term treasury bond that is sold at a discount and may be redeemed at full face value for payment of federal estate taxes in the event of death of the owner. *Also called* flower bond.

Eurobond: A corporate bond issued through international markets for which interest and principal are payable in the currency in which the bond is issued.

Eurodollar: United States dollars held on deposit and circulated among bank and financial institutions throughout the world that are used for short-term trade financing.

European depository receipt: (EDR): Similar to American depository receipt. An EDR is a certificate issued in place of shares of a firm located in another country to simplify international trading of securities.

even spread: A spread position in which the investor neither receives nor pays a premium. The premium received from the long position will equal the premium owed on the short position.

ex: Without, as in ex-dividend.

excess profits: A corporation's profits that the government has determined to be excessive, based on some historical base period.

excess profits tax: A federal income tax imposed on corporate profits that have been determined excessive.

excess reserves: Deposits held by member banks of the Federal Reserve System that are above the minimum requirements set by the Federal Reserve Board.

exchange: (1) The physical location where buyers and sellers are brought together to transact business. (2) A physical location where brokers and dealers transact security business for their clients. (3) The transfer of funds, property, or services for other funds, property, or services. (4) The transfer of the legal currency of one country for the legal currency of another country.

exchange acquisition: A method used to execute a buy order for a large block of stock in which several sell orders are placed together and crossed with the buy order on the floor of the exchange.

exchange distribution: A method used to execute a sell order for a large block of stock in which several buy orders are placed together and crossed with the sell order on the floor of the exchange.

exchange floor: The actual area of a stock exchange where security trading between brokers and dealers takes place.

exchange option contract: *See* listed option.

exchange rate: The rate at which one currency can be exchanged for another.

exchange seat: Membership on a stock exchange. Membership is required to transact business on any exchange. Seats are limited in number and are sold on the open market if a member leaves a particular exchange.

ex-dividend: Without dividend. For example, a stock is trading after ex-dividend date but before payment date of the current dividend. The person buying the stock on or after ex-dividend date is not entitled to the current dividend; and the person selling the stock before ex-dividend is not entitled to the dividend.

ex-dividend date: The date on which a stock starts trading without the dividend. This is usually four days before the date of record. Owners of record prior to the ex-dividend date are entitled to the dividend.

execution: The completion of instructions given by an investor to buy or sell securities. The filling of a buy or sell order.

exercise: (1) To exchange a right or warrant (plus any money due) for its equivalent in stock. (2) The procedure by which the holder of an option contract notifies the writer of the contract that he wishes to buy or sell shares of the underlying security. This is done through the brokerage firm which must tender an exercise notice to the Options Clearing Corporation.

exercise assignment: Notification to the writer of a stock option contract that the option has been exercised against him.

exercise cut-off time: The time, set by the exchanges, by which option holders must notify their brokerage firms that they wish to exercise their options. Currently, the cut-off time is 5:30 p.m. Eastern time on the business day preceding the expiration date.

exercise limit: Rule of the option exchanges stating that no investor or group of investors acting together may exercise more than 2,000 options for each class, within five consecutive days.

exercise notification: *See* exercise assignment.

exercise price: The price per share at which the holder of a stock option contract may purchase the underlying security on a call option, or sell the underlying security on a put option. *Also called* strike price, striking price.

exhaustion gap: A price gap that ends or reverses a previous trend. *See* gap.

ex-interest: Without interest. For example, a bond is trading on or after ex-interest date but before payment date of the current interest payment. The buyer of the bond is not entitled to the current interest payment.

expiration cycle: The set of months during which listed options may trade. There are three expiration cycles, and options contracts on the same underlying security may trade in only one of the three cycles. First cycle: January, April, July, October. Second cycle: February, May, August, November. Third cycle: March, June, September, December.

expiration date: (1) The date on which securities of value such as rights or warrants expire and are no longer of value. (2) The latest date a listed stock option contract may be exercised before it expires, which is currently the Saturday following the third Friday of the expiration month.

expiration month: The month in which a stock option contract expires.

expiration time: The latest time a listed stock option contract may be exercised before it expires, which is currently 11:59 a.m. Eastern time on the expiration date.

expire: To lapse. A right, warrant, or stock option contract that becomes worthless because it was not exercised within the specific time period allowed.

ex-rights date: The date on which the buyer of common stock is not entitled to the rights that had been declared for the stock. Typically this is the first business day after the effective date of the statement of registration.

ex-rights: Without rights. For example, a security on which rights have been declared but not yet issued is now trading without those rights attached; therefore the buyer will not receive any rights.

extended: An advance or decline in the price of a security that extends the previously established trend and suggests a high probability that a subsequent consolidation will occur.

extra dividend: A dividend paid in addition to the normally declared annual dividend amount. This is not an increase in the annual dividend payment and there is no guarantee it will be paid again. *Also called* special dividend.

ex-warrant: Without warrants. When an issue that was trading with warrants begins trading without those warrants attached, the seller has retained ownership of the warrants.

face-amount certificate company (FAC): One type of investment company which issues only debt securities that pay a fixed guaranteed rate of return.

face value: The value that is printed or stamped on the face of an instrument of value. The face value may have little relation to the market value of an instrument. Face value may also be called par value. For most bonds, face value represents the value of the bond at maturity. Current market value will usually vary from face value. *See* par value.

fails: The inability of a broker or dealer to settle his trades with another broker or dealer by settlement date.

failures: Organizations that voluntarily or involuntarily do not remain in business—usually due to financial or managerial problems.

fair market value: The price at which buyers and sellers are willing to trade when both have complete information and neither has unusual leverage over the other. There is fair and sufficient disclosure and all rules are followed by both parties.

fair return: (1) The amount of profit or income one should hope to receive on an investment, taking into consideration the amount invested and risk involved. (2) The approved profit of

regulated industries such as telephone, gas, and electric.

fall-out-of-bed: Term used to describe a market that suddenly falls far below recent levels.

Fannie Mae: Common nickname for Federal National Mortgage Association.

far option: That side of a stock spread option position that expires after the other side. *See* spread. *Compare* near option.

FDIC: *See* Federal Deposit Insurance Corporation.

Fed: Nickname for the Federal Reserve System and in particular for the Federal Reserve Board.

Federal Deposit Insurance Corporation: A government sponsored corporation that insures accounts in national banks and other qualified institutions. At the present time over 90 percent of all commercial banks and 60 percent of all mutual savings banks are insured through the FDIC.

federal funds: Funds in excess of Federal Reserve requirements that are traded among member banks on a short-term—usually day-to-day—basis.

Federal funds rate: The interest rate charged on funds that member banks of the Federal Reserve System borrow from each other. Banks in this well-organized market holding reserves in excess of the legal requirements offer to lend them on a day-to-day basis to other member banks.

Federal Home Loan Mortgage Corporation (FHLMC): Commonly called Freddie Mac. A government sponsored corporation that was established to develop a secondary market in conventional residential mortgages. Its function is to buy mortgages from financial institutions that have their deposits or accounts insured by an agency of the federal government and then resell those mortgages in pools and by issuing notes and bonds which are publically traded.

Federal National Mortgage Association (FNMA): Commonly called Fannie Mae. The FNMA was originally established as a government sponsored corporation to give assistance for mortgages. Today it is a privately owned corporation of the U.S. government whose primary function is to buy and resell government insured or guaranteed single-family mortgages to lessen cyclical patterns. It issues short-term notes, bonds, and stocks which are traded on the exchanges.

Federal Reserve Bank reserve requirement: Stated as a percentage of demand deposits, it is the amount of uninvested funds member banks are required to hold in reserve either in cash or on deposit with the Federal Reserve System.

Federal Reserve Board: The board of governors that administers the Federal Reserve System. It is made up of members appointed by the President of the United States and confirmed by the Senate. Its primary duty is to supervise all operations of the Federal Reserve System including the Federal Reserve Banks, member banks, the Open Market Committee, and the Federal Advisory Council. In addition, it sets current market margin requirements, bank reserve requirements, the discount rate, and the execution of the open market operations. Address: 20th Street and Constitution Avenue N.W., Washington, D.C. 20006.

Federal Reserve discount rate: The interest rate charged on funds tht member banks borrow directly from any Federal Reserve District Bank. The rate is set by the Federal Reserve Board. In general, when the Federal Reserve Board feels that expansion of credit and money should be encouraged in the public interest, it reduces the discount rate. When the Fed believes expansion should be halted, it raises the discount rate.

Federal Reserve note: The prevalent form of paper currency in circulation in the United States. These notes are issued by a Federal Reserve Bank in denominations varying from $1 to $10,000.

Federal Reserve System: Created by an Act of Congress, the Federal Reserve System influences the policies by which both the banking system and the monetary systems are controlled. It consists of 12 Federal Reserve Districts, each with its own Federal Reserve Bank, along with the Federal Open Market Committee and the board of governors.

Federal Savings and Loan Insurance Corporation (FSLIC): Government sponsored corporation that insures certain accounts in all federal savings and loan associations and approved state savings and loan associations.

Federation Internationale des Bourses de Valeurs (FIBV): The international Federation of Stock Exchanges, headquartered in Paris, France. The FIBV helps determine policies that permit international financial investing. The New York Stock Exchange is a member of this association.

fiat money: Paper currency and coins that are backed by the full faith and credit of the issuing government rather than some standard such as gold. All U.S. paper currency and coins are fiat money.

fiduciary: A person or institution who holds a relationship of trust in a financial capacity when acting for another; in particular, where he holds, administers, invests and/or distributes funds in whole or part for another party.

FIFO: *See* first-in, first-out.

fill or kill order (FOK): A market or limit order with trading instructions (qualifier) that the order is to be executed in its entirety as soon as it reaches the trading post or desk. If the order is not immediately executed in its entirety, it is automatically canceled.

finance: To raise or provide funds for capital by issuing stock, bonds, or notes. (2) The system that includes the circulation of money, lending, investments, and banking operations.

financial expense: The cost directly associated with financing a business such as bond interest payments.

financial futures: Contracts traded on financial instruments (such as Treasury bills) that are to be delivered in the future. The contract states the price, interest rate, terms, and delivery date.

financial planning: Evaluating one's financial needs and objectives to determine short-term and long-term financial needs, investment strategy, insurance needs, and estate planning.

financial statements: Various reports issued periodically by corporations to shareholders and analysts giving information on corporate financial status. These include the Statement of Income and Retained Earnings, the Balance Sheet, and the Statement of Change in Financial Position. The statements are issued on a quarterly basis and at fiscal year-end.

fineness: The purity of precious metal in a coin or ingot. The degree of fineness is stated as a percentage of total content. For example, a gold coin may be 80 percent fine, which means the coin is made up of 80 percent pure gold and 20 percent other metals.

firm maintenance excess: The on-going minimum equity requirement of the long market value of margined securities. Most firms use a maintenance requirement of 30 percent.

firm market: A price that is either not negotiable or minimally negotiable. See firm price.

firm order: Verbal or written instruction given by an investor to a broker to buy or sell a stated number of shares of a particular security, either at market price or at a specific limit price. This may also include certain specific trading instructions.

firm price: Price quoted by a securities dealer that is not negotiable or only minimally negotiable and is quoted for that particular time only. The price may change depending on market conditions. Compare subject price.

first-in, first-out (FIFO): (1) An inventory evaluation method in which the cost of earliest material received is assumed to be the first used. (2) IRS evaluation method used in partial liquidation of securities or mutual fund shares when more than one purchase of the security is involved. The earliest purchases are assumed to be the first to be sold unless otherwise stipulated at the time of sale.

first mortgage bond: A long-term debt instrument that is secured by a first mortgage on all or part of the property of the issuer.

fiscal policy: The government policies for spending and taxation and increasing or decreasing regulations to accomplish their present economic goals.

fiscal year: A twelve-month accounting and taxation period based on either the calendar year or the natural business year of a corporation.

five percent policy: See NASDAQ 5 percent policy.

fixed annuity: A tax-deferred, interest-bearing insurance product for which the annuitant deposits a set sum of money for future income payments. Many purchase methods and annuity options are available. Major advantages are: (a) safety of principal, (b) tax-deferred interest, (c) exclusion from probate.

fixed assets: For accounting purposes, these are tangible assets that are more or less permanent in nature, such as land, buildings, and machinery.

fixed expenses: Recurring costs and charges—such as rent, interest and administrative costs—that have no direct relationship to the volume of business activity.

fixed income investment: An investment that pays a stated fixed rate of return throughout its duration. For example, until their maturity, bonds pay a fixed rate of interest, which is stated as a percentage of face value.

fixed return dividend: A dividend that will neither increase nor decrease throughout time. This is typical in the case of preferred stocks.

flag: A charted stock pattern that represents a plateau in prices.

flash reporting: (1) A method major exchanges use when transaction reporting falls six minutes behind the market activity. Instead of normal reporting, every five minutes prices of 15 stocks are given. These up-to-the-minute prices are preceded by the word FLASH. (2) A news or financial release that gives highlights of a story which will be followed by a complete report.

flat: Term used to indicate that a bond is trading with no allowance for accrued interest. The seller does not receive nor does the buyer pay accrued interest from the last interest payment date. Bonds trade flat (without accured interest) if they are income bonds, if settlement date is the same as coupon payment date, or if the bonds are in default. *Compare* full.

flat income bond: Income bonds that are trading with no allowance for accrued interest. *See* income bond.

float: (1) To issue a security offering. (2) The quantity of a particular security that is available for trading. (3) The difference between outgoing and incoming funds. (4) Uncollected deposits that have been credited by a bank to its customers' accounts.

floating interest rate: A variable interest rate that is adjusted with the movement of other market and economic conditions, but especially with the rate of Treasury bills and the prime rate. The rate is typically adjusted every quarter.

floating rate bonds: Debt instruments issued by large corporations and financial institutions on which the interest rate is pegged to another rate (typically the Treasury bill rate) and periodically adjusted at a specified amount over that rate. Adjustments are made either quarterly, semiannually or annually. Some issues allow the holder the right to "put" or redeem the notes to the issuer at par value before maturity date.

floating rate preferred stock: Preferred stock on which the dividend rate is pegged to the Treasury bill rate or some other rate and periodically adjusted at some set amount over that rate.

floating supply: The number of shares of a given security that are usually available in the market for trading. All shares issued and outstanding are not included in the float—just those normally available for trading.

floor: The area of a stock exchange where security trading actually takes place.

floor broker: Member of an exchange who executes buy and sell orders on the floor. The transactions may represent trades for clients of his own firm or for those of other brokers. *Also called* commission house broker.

floor partner: A partner or officer of an exchange member firm who handles transactions for his own firm on the trading floor.

floor trader: A registered member of an exchange who trades only for his own account and those in which he has an interest.

flower bond: A long-term government bond that may be redeemed at par value when the proceeds are used to pay federal estate taxes if owned by the decedent at the time of death. This special tax treatment is generally no longer in effect. *Also called* estate tax bond.

fluctuation: The movement of a security's market price that occurs from one transaction to the next. These changes are reported in points (one dollar equals one point) and fractions of a point. Fluctuations in price occur due to supply and demand factors at any given time.

flurry: A temporary sharp increase in the trading volume of a stock. Such activity is usually the result of a news story or some other published information.

FNMA: *See* Federal National Mortgage Association.

forecast: (1) To predict future market price and/or volume trends by using various analytical data. (2) To estimate future sales, costs and earnings of a business.

foreclosure: Legal process in which mortgage holders take possession of property when there is a default on payments. The property is usually auctioned in order to reimburse mortgage holders.

foreign buy/sell ratio: Total foreign buying of U.S. securities divided by total foreign selling of U.S. securities. This indicator is used to measure sentiment abroad toward the U.S. markets.

foreign corporation: (1) In state laws, it is a corporation created under the laws of another state or country. (2) In federal law, it is a corporation created under the laws of another country. *Compare* domestic corporation.

foreign currency: Paper money and coins in circulation and used as a medium of exchange in a country other than one's own. Those most often traded in

international money markets include:

Argentina	peso
Australia	dollar
Austria	schilling
Belgium	franc
Brazil	cruzeiro
Canada	dollar
China, People's Republic	yuan
China, Republic of	dollar
Colombia	peso
Denmark	krone
Ecuador	sucre
Finland	markka
France	franc
Germany, East	mark
Germany, West	deutsche mark
Greece	drachma
India	rupee
Ireland	pound
Israel	pound
Italy	lira
Japan	yen
Lebanon	pound
Malaysia	ringgit
Mexico	peso
Netherlands	guilder
New Zealand	dollar
Norway	krone
Pakistan	rupee
Peru	sol
Philippines	peso
Portugal	escudo
Saudi Arabia	riyal
Singapore	dollar
South Africa	rand
Spain	peseta
Sweden	krona
Switzerland	franc
United Kingdom	pound
Venezuela	bolivar

foreign exchange: The process of handling and settling international transactions. International trade results in large amounts of currency that must be physically moved or credited from one nation to another.

foreign exchange rate: The value of one nation's currency in relation to others. The rate is the number of units of one currency that may be exchanged for one unit of another currency.

51

form 10-K: An annual report that all corporations having securities registered under the laws of the Securities Exchange Act of 1934 must release and make available to the public.

formula investing: Various investment approaches in which the investor buys and sells securities according to a predetermined plan. Formula plans are conservative and help simplify the investing process. They can be based on investing a set dollar amount at regular intervals; buying/selling at predetermined price levels; and so on. The most widely used formula plan are dollar cost averaging, constant ratio investing, and variable ratio investing.

forward buying: A term used in commodity trading that indicates investors are buying at present market prices for delivery in the future while anticipating higher price movements.

forward market: Any market in which transactions are handled at present market prices but call for delivery in the future. Commodity futures, stock options and currency exchange markets are all of this nature.

forward selling: A term used in commodity trading that indicates investors are selling at present market prices for delivery in the future while anticipating lower price movements.

foundation: A non-profit private organization with a tax-free status that takes in and distributes funds for charitable and other approved causes.

founders' shares: Capital stock issued to founding members for their efforts in setting up a corporation. These shares carry special restrictions in most cases.

fourth market: A computerized system (Instinet) that allows subscribers to indicate their interest in purchasing or selling blocks of stock or bonds and to complete their transactions without the aid of any broker or dealer. *See* Instinet.

fractional share: Any portion that is less than one whole share. This may occur in stock splits, stock dividends, dividend reinvestments, monthly investment plans, and share building plans.

Freddie Mac: *See* Federal Home Loan Mortgage Corporation.

free market: A market in which price is a function of supply and demand factors rather than being regulated.

free ride: (1) Illegal practice where a person places a buy order with a broker and if the stock moves up significantly in price sells the stock before payment is due on the purchase. In that way, the person receives a profit without putting any money at risk. (2) Illegal practice where a dealer will keep a portion of a desirable issue for personal investment or for favored clients instead of offering those shares openly to the public.

Friedman, Milton: Economist whose monetarism theory states that a nation's monetary controls will affect economic conditions. The theory states that the nation's economy moves in the same direction as the expanding or contracting money supply.

front-end commission: *See* front-end load.

front-end load: A sales charge placed on many mutual funds at the start of the contract to purchase shares. The average sales charge is about 6 to 8 percent. However, most mutual funds offer a discount on increased dollar purchases.

front running: Illegal practice in which an option client will act on information that has not yet been transmitted on the tape of the exchange where the underlying security is traded. For example, if the option client learns that a large block of stock has been bought or sold but is not yet reported on the tape, the client will buy or sell options based on this information.

full: Indication that a bond is trading with accrued interest. The seller receives and the buyer pays all accrued interest from last payment date up to but not including settlement date. *Compare* flat.

full disclosure: The process of revealing all material and pertinent facts about an organization, its financial status, management, any litigations, and use of the proceeds from a public offering. Full disclosure is required in a public stock or bond offering.

full faith and credit: Promise to pay a contractual debt that is backed by the creditworthiness of the issuing party rather than any collateral.

full faith and credit bond: The financial obligation of a municipality or division that is not backed by any collateral other than the creditworthiness of the municipality. It is a direct obligation of the municipality.

full service funds: Mutual funds that allow shareholders to have their capital gains and dividends automatically reinvested in additional shares of that fund.

full trading authorization: Approval for someone other than the brokerage client to have trading authority in the client's account. This includes purchases, sales and withdrawal of funds and securities.

fully invested: A situation where an individual investor or institutional investor has all or basically all available cash invested and therefore cannot make additional investments unless some present investment is liquidated.

fully managed funds: Mutual funds and/or other investment companies that are allowed by their charter to invest in more than one specific type of investments. According to market conditions they will invest in common stocks, bonds, preferred stocks or a combination.

fully paid securities: Those securities for which the investor has paid in full, not bought on margin or hypothecated.

fund: (1) To supply capital for an enterprise. (2) Common term used for mutual fund.

fundamental analysis: Examination and interpretation of all relevant factors that can influence the direction of a corporation's growth, earnings and dividends. This includes the analysis of economic data, industry conditions, company fundamentals and corporate financial statements. *Compare* technical analysis.

fundamental analyst: A securities analyst who examines and interprets all factors that influence the direction of corporate growth and then makes forecasts and market recommendations based on this information. *Compare* technical analyst.

fundamentalist: Investor who places emphasis on the fundmental conditions of a corporation and the economy rather than the technical factors of the market or a particular security.

funded debt: Capital raised by the issuance of long-term debt instruments such as bond and long-term notes.

futures: Contracts to buy or sell based on prevailing market prices with delivery or receipt set at a specific future date. This includes stock options, commodity markets, international currency exchange markets, and markets for trading financial instruments. If the market price should change between contract date and delivery date, it will result in a profit or loss to the trader depending on the contract.

futures exchange: An organized exchange for trading futures contracts.

future value of a dollar: The amount by which $1 will grow at a given rate of interest if compounded for a specified number of periods.

gain: The realized or unrealized profit on an invesment.

galloping inflation: Phrase used to describe an inflationary situation that cannot be controlled by normal means.

gambling: Taking a risk without fully investigating the facts or investing capital on the basis of a hunch or whim.

gap: A price movement in which a stock's high and low prices have no overlap with the previous day's high and low prices. Gaps are used in measuring enthusiasm of buying or selling for a particular stock. Gaps also measure illiquidity in certain issues.

general management investment company: A mutual fund or other investment company that is not restricted to any special type of investment, but may diversify its investments according to market conditions. *Also called Fully Managed Fund.*

general mortgage bond: A debt instrument backed by a blanket mortgage on all or most of the issuing company's property even though that property may already have an existing mortgage.

general obligation bond (GO): A debt instrument issued by a municipality backed by the full faith, credit and taxing power of the issuer. Most state,

city, and county bonds are GOs, but limited tax bonds and special assessment bonds are included in this general category.

general partnership: An unincorporated business organization formed by two or more persons. Each partner shares in the profits according to a predetermined plan and each has unlimited liability.

Gifts to Minors Act: State-by-state laws that permit adults (not necessarily the parent) to act as custodians of an investment account for a minor, and that do not require a court appointment. All money and purchases of stock are considered gifts and may not be rescinded. All purchases, sales, dividends, and interest are made in the name of the minor.

gilt edged: High grade securities issued by corporations that have a proven record for profit and payment of dividends and interest over many years.

Ginnie Mae: Common nickname for Government National Mortgage Association.

give-up: The splitting of a commission when one broker executes an order on behalf of another broker's client. The client pays the normal commission which is then divided between the two brokers.

glamour stocks: Issues that have captured investors' enthusiasm because they believe the issue will increase in value more quickly than other stocks, industries, or the general market. These issues usually sell at high price/earnings ratios and above current projected potential.

Glass-Steagal Act of 1933: Federal act that prohibited commercial banks from underwriting or dealing in corporate securities.

GNMA: *See* Government National Mortgage Association.

GNP: The total value of all goods and services produced in this country for a specific time period. *See* gross national product.

GO: *See* general obligation bond.

go-go fund: Mutual fund that concentrates its investments in speculative common stocks in anticipation of making short-term high profits.

gold certificate: Legal tender that is backed by gold and may be converted into gold on demand. Today most major currencies are backed by the full faith and credit of the issuing government rather than by gold.

gold fix: The setting of the price of gold by dealers.

gold shares: Issues of companies engaged primarily in gold-mining activities.

go long: General term meaning to buy stock in anticipation of a price increase or to cover a short position.

good delivery: Presenting a security certificate in proper form in order to transfer title in the completion of a security transaction. Requirements are that (1) the certificate be in good condition (2) the certificate be properly endorsed in the proper place (3) the certificate belong to the person making the transaction and (4) any additional legal document that may be required accompany the certificate.

good faith deposit: A deposit that may be required on the first and/or second transaction when establishing an account with a brokerage firm. This is done when the investor's credit is unknown to the brokerage firm. Typically, the deposit is 25 percent of the purchase price.

good quality: Based on fundamental information, this term describes securities issued by corporations with good financial status, who are known for satisfactory payment of dividends and interest over a long period and have above average standing in their industry.

good until canceled order (GTC): An order to buy or sell a stated number of shares of a specific security that remains in effect until it is executed or canceled by the investor. In some firms, GTC orders are renewed every 30 days or every quarter. *Also called open order.*

go private: The process of changing a public corporation to one that is privately held. This involves buying back the outstanding shares of stock in accordance with SEC regulations.

go public: The process of bringing a privately-held corporation into one that is publicly held. This involves registration with the Securities and Exchange Commission and meeting certain requirements.

go short: To sell stock that one does not own in anticipation of a decline in the price of that security. *See* short sale.

government agency securities: Debt securities issued by various agencies of the federal government, such as Government National Mortgage Associations. Most agency securities, unlike treasury issues, are not guaranteed by the federal government.

government bills: Debt securities issued by the U.S. federal government that mature in one year or less.

government bonds: Long-term debt securities issued by the U.S. federal government or any agency of the federal government. These are the highest rate bonds available.

Governmental National Mortgage Association (GNMA): Commonly called Ginnie Mae. A government sponsored corporation administered through the Department of Housing and Urban Development. GNMA buys mortgages in areas that have difficulty in securing financing and then resells these mortgages in packages to investors. The minimum investment is normally $25,000 and the investors receive payment of principal and interest.

government notes: Debt securities issued by the United States federal government or any agency of the federal government. These notes usually mature in two to ten years, provide excellent safety and are easily traded.

grading of securities: Assessment of securities according to management ability, financial strength, stability and other corporate information and comparisons to similar securities.

Great Depression: The economic depression that affected almost every nation which began with the stock market crash of October 29, 1929 and continued until the mid 1930s.

gross: The total sum before deductions are taken. For example, gross sales, gross profits.

gross national product (GNP): The market value of final goods and services produced by the nation's economy within a specific time period. GNP and its major components are key elements of economic forecasting. Its components measure consumer, government and business spending.

gross profit: (1) The profit an investor receives before allowing for commissions, taxes or other deductions. (2) In accounting, it is the profit after subtracting the cost of goods sold and overhead, but before taxes.

gross spread: The fee the underwriter will charge the seller on the sale of a secondary distribution (resale of a large block of stock). The spread includes the underwriting commission, the manager's fee and the selling concession.

group averages: The average of market prices, price/earnings ratios, earnings per share, and so on for a group of companies within a particular industry.

growth fund: A mutual fund that invests primarily in shares of common stock of corporations that are believed to be growing faster than other companies, industries, or the market as a whole. These shares are expected to increase rapidly in value.

growth industry: An industry or business that appears to be increasing in both sales and earnings, with continued growth expected. Some industries that have at various times been classified as growth industries include aerospace, electronics, mobile homes, medical research laboratories, and high technology companies.

growth portfolio: A portfolio of securities comprised of common stocks that are expected to give rapid appreciation rather than current income.

growth stock: Securities issued by companies whose sales and earnings are expanding faster than the economy and/or faster than the average of their particular industry. Profits are typically reinvested into the companies, and therefore shareholders receive small dividends or no dividends at all.

GTC: *See* good until cancelled order.

guaranteed account: A brokerage account that is guaranteed by another client. Equity in the guarantor's account may be used for the guaranteed account and this guarantee must be in writing and signed by the guarantor.

guarantee mortgage certificate: A pass-through security representing an undivided interest in a package of conventional mortgages that the Federal Home Loan Mortgage Corporation has purchased. *See* Federal Home Loan Mortgage Corporation.

guaranteed bond: A long-term debt obligation issued by one corporation that is guaranteed by another corporation—for example, a parent company.

half-hedged option: Stock-option writing strategy in which the option writer sells two option contracts for every 100 shares of the underlying security that are owned.

handling charge: A special charge some brokerage firms impose for handling small orders.

head and shoulders: A charted price pattern. A series of peaks with the central peak being higher than the previous or following peaks. It may be interpreted as a sell signal and the end of an upward trend.

hedge: (1) The practice of offsetting or minimizing a possible loss in one investment. For example, to offset a loss in a particular stock, the investor may sell that same stock short. (2) The practice of using speculative moves to increase profits. For example, to margin paper profits.

hedged fund: An unregulated investment fund in which speculative investments, such as margin, short selling, trading futures contacts, and buying and selling puts and calls are used to achieve its objectives of using relatively small amounts of cash to make quick profits.

hedger: One who makes equal investments simultaneously in alternative investments in an attempt to minimize the risks stemming from fluctuations in prices, and in order to profit from those fluctuations.

heavy industry: Basic industries, such as the steel and mining industries.

hidden inflation: A reduction in the quality or value of goods and services sold that may be accompanied by a small increase in price. Hidden inflation does not show up in any price indexes, yet it does affect the economy.

high: In security prices, it is the highest price that was reached during any specified time period. It may be the high for the day, the month, or the year.

high flier: A speculative situation where a stock is increasing in value very rapidly and its market price is usually not justified based on current expected earnings of the company.

high/low index: An index showing yearly highs and lows on a moving average basis. It is used as a market breadth indicator and used to predict major trend changes.

high quality securities: Based on fundamental information, this describes an investment opportunity in which the corporation has strong financial status and management, an excellent interest and dividend payment record over a long period of time, and high standing in its industry.

high-risk securities: Based on fundamental information, this describes an investment situation with a strong possibility of price volatility. The companies may be new, based on one product, or headed by unproven management. The price/earnings ratios are typically very high and the capital structure is usually small.

high tech: A high technology company producing goods or providing services in complex technological processess such as computers.

hit the bid: Execution of an order given by an investor to sell a security at the current bid price (which is the current highest price anyone is willing to pay) rather than negotiate a higher price or accept a lower price.

hold: (1) To own a stock or bond or other instrument of value. (2) To have the intention of owning for a long period of time rather than short-term trading.

holder: The option client who has purchased a contract giving him the right either to buy the underlying security in the case of a call or to sell the security in the case of a put, at a predetermined price, and within a specified period of time. *Also called* buyer.

holding company: A corporation with a policy of acquiring or controlling other companies. Usually these companies are in related industries.

holding page: Client account record maintained by the brokerage firm that shows all buy and sell transactions and current holdings.

holding period: The period during which an investment or other asset is owned. The holding period is used to determine whether a profit or loss is classified as long-term or short-term and to determine whether sales of securities are wash sale transactions.

holding the market: Purhasing shares of stock that are being heavily sold to prevent a severe decline in price. This may be done by specialists and/or major shareholders of a corporation. Immediately after a new offering, the underwriter will often hold the market to keep the current market price at or near the original offering price.

Honolulu Stock Exchange: Address: 843 Fort Street, Honolulu, Hawaii 96813.

horizontal bear spread: A spread option position that involves the purchase and sale of options within the same class whereby the option purchased will have a closer expiration date than the option that is sold. *Also called* calendar bear spread. *Compare* horizontal bull spread.

horizontal bull spread: A spread option position that involves the purchase and sale of options within the same class, whereby the option that is sold will have a closer expiration date than the option that is purchased. *Also called* calendar bull spread. *Compare* horizontal bear spread.

horizontal spread: A spread option strategy that involves the purchase and sale of option contracts that are within the same class and on the same underlying security, and have the same striking (exercise) price, but that have different expiration dates. *Also called* time spread, calendar spread. *Compare* vertical spread.

hot issue: A new issue of stock that has tremendous public demand. Demand exceeds supply and the stock begins trading at high multiples immediately after completion of the initial offering.

house account: (1) The trading account of a brokerage firm using funds of the partners. (2) A client's account that is directly handled by a partner of the brokerage firm rather than an employed registered representative.

house maintenance call: Request by a brokerage firm for a client to put up additional money or securities when the equity in the margin account falls below the firm's minimum maintenance requirement.

house maintenance requirement: The minimum equity that must be maintained in a margin account according to each individual brokerage firm's rules. Most firms have a minimum maintenance requirement of 30 percent.

hyperinflation: High rate of inflation that is out of control and cannot be handled by normal government policies.

hypothecated stock: Securities that have been pledged as collateral for a loan.

hypothecation agreement: Document signed by clients who open margin accounts that allows pledging of securities for the purposed of borrowing funds against securities.

hypothecation: Pledging securities as collateral to obtain either a loan from a bank or margin privileges in a brokerage account.

identified shares: Particular shares, from a multiple holding of the same security purchased at different prices, that the client identifies as being the shares that are to be sold. This is often done to show a short-term capital loss or long-term capital gain on the sale of securities for tax accounting purposes.

IDR: *See* international depository receipt.

illiquid: (1) Having insufficient liquid assets (cash or cash equivalents) to meet short-term obligations. (2) An investment that cannot be easily or quickly turned into cash.

immediate or cancel order: Similar to a fill or kill order. An order to buy or sell with trading instructions (qualifier) that the order is to be executed immediately in whole or part as soon as it is presented to the trading floor. Unlike a fill or kill order, partial execution is acceptable to the investor. Any portion not immediately filled is automatically canceled.

inactive account: A brokerage account with little or no activity over a period of several months.

inactive post: A trading post on the floor of the New York Stock Exchange where infrequently traded securities are handled. *Also called* post 30.

inactive stock: A stock in which there is relatively small trading volume. These are usually traded on the over-the-counter market, but may be handled at the inactive post on the New York Stock Exchange.

in-and-out trade: A security purchase that is followed by an immediate sale with the intention of making an immediate short-term profit.

income: (1) Personal or business revenues received for a particular period. (2) The funds received from an investment in the form of interest or dividends.

income bond: A bond that has a stated rate of interest with principal due at maturity; however, the interest is payable only as earned by the corporation.

income fund: A mutual fund in which the primary objective is high current income for the shareholders rather than growth in principal.

income property: Real property investment that is used as a source of income—such as rental property.

income bond: A bond that has a stated rate of interest with principal due at maturity; however, the interest is payable only as earned by the corporation.

income fund: A mutual fund in which the primary objective is high current income for the shareholders rather than growth in principal.

income property: Real property investment that is used as a source of income—such as rental property.

income portfolio: Security holdings of individual or institutional investors that are designed to give high current income rather than emphasize growth of capital.

income statement: An accounting statement showing profit or loss for a business orgainization for a specified period of time.

income stocks: Issues that pay a higher than average current return. High-yielding dividend stocks that are considered a conservative investment.

incorporation: The legal process of becoming a chartered corporation. *See* corporation.

indenture: The legal instrument under which terms of a debenture are stated—specifying the principal amount, maturity date, interest rate, any qualifications and duties of the trustee, and the rights and obligations of the issuers and the holders.

index: A statistical measurement usually expressed in terms of a percentage of a base period, used to measure price and/or performance.

indexing: An investment technique that attempts to organize and weight its holdings so that it will perform much as a specific major stock index performs.

Index of Industrial Production: A federally maintained index that measures and compares changes in the actual output of the nation's industries, mining operations, and utility production. This is a coincident indicator that helps to verify market moves and is one of the key tools in measuring the health of the economy.

index options: Option contracts, issued by the Options Clearing Corporation, which are based on a stock index rather than an underlying security. When exercised, settlement is made by the payment of cash—not delivery of shares.

indicated market: A qualified (subject) price on a security that must be confirmed before an order is executed. *Compare* firm market.

indicated yield: The estimated yield on a stock for a given time period (usually 12 months) based on current and projected dividend payments.

indication of interest (IOI): Orders taken to purchase shares of a new offering that are not firm commitments to buy. These orders are taken during the period prior to final registration and must either be canceled or confirmed once the final prospectus is completed.

indicators: Quantitative factors that show with more or less exactness a correlation to stock market trends or economic trends. These are used to project future market movements. *See* economic indicators, leading indicators, coincident indicators, lagging indicators.

individual retirement account (IRA): A tax-favored, self-funded retirement plan approved by the Internal Revenue Service that allows most employed individuals to contribute, up to a set maximum amount, toward their retirement on a tax-deferred basis. The allowance is currently *the lesser of* $2,000 or 100 percent of earned income. *See* Keogh.

indorsee: The person to whom a negotiable instrument is transferred by endorsement.

indorsor: The person who signs a negotiable instrument in order to transfer title from himself to another.

industrial average: *See* Dow Jones Industrial Average.

industrial bond: Term used to describe any of the long-term financial debt obligations issued by corporations other than utilities, banks, and railroads. The proceeds are used for expansion, working capital, and/or to retire other debts.

industrial development bond: A tax-exempt municipal bond that is issued by an authority of a state, city, or municipality to finance facilities for private business in order to attract industry. The principal and interest is paid from revenue generated by leases on this property. *Also called* industrial revenue bond.

industrial stocks: Common stock issued by industrial corporations rather than utilities, banks, or railroads.

industrials: *See* Dow Jones Industrial Average.

industry: (1) Firms engaged in manufacturing, molding, processing, printing, refining, and extracting. (2) Term generally used to indicate a defined segment of business. For example, advertising, banking, and restaurants are all referred to a separate industries.

industry funds: Mutual funds that are designed to place the majority of their investments in preferred stocks and bonds of industrial companies, seeking high yields and preservation of capital.

inflation: An increase in prices, costs, and wages accompanied by a decrease in the purchasing power of money.

inflationary gap: Often thought to set the pace of inflation, this gap is the difference between investment funds available both from private and public sectors and the total amount of savings.

inflationary risk: The risk that an investment will have less purchasing power when it is liquidated than when originally invested.

inflation hedge: An investment that is projected to increase in value at a rate that will at least offset the decline in purchasing power of the dollar in a period of inflation. Some investments will increase in value as inflation increases, others will decline.

initial equity: The amount of money or securities required to open a margin account. *See* initial margin.

initial margin: The funds a customer must deposit in a margin account when originating a long or short position. Currently the amount is 50 percent of the purchase price or 50 percent of the market value from a short sale, with a minimum requirement of $2,000. The initial margin requirement goes into effect for each purchase or short sale. *See* maintenance margin requirement, margin.

inside information: Material facts about the conditions and plans of a corporation that have not been released to employees or the general public.

insider: A director, officer, or benefical owner of 10 percent or more of any class of security of a corporation or other persons having corporate information that is not available to the general public.

insider buying: Purchases of stock by officials and other key persons of a corporation in their publicly traded corporation.

insider selling: Selling of stock by officials and other key persons of a corporation in their publicly traded corporation.

insider transaction: The buying or selling of stock by officers, major stockholders, or other key persons in a corporation. The SEC requires that such transactions be reported within ten days after the close of the month in which the transactions are made. Often, if insiders are buying heavily it is considered bullish and if they are selling it is considered bearish.

INSTINET: Institutional Networks Corporation. A computerized service that enables subscribers to complete transactions in the "fourth market" without brokerage firm or dealer involvement.

institutional brokerage firm: Those firms that specialize in servicing the needs of the institutional investor.

institutional buy/sell ratio: Institutional buying divided by institutional selling, which measures the degree of enthusiasm or pessimism among institutional investors.

institutional investors: Financial institutions such as banks, insurance companies, mutual funds, pension funds, and so on, that buy and sell large blocks of securities. It is estimated that they hold 70-80 percent of all securities being traded.

instrument: Any document that confers a right or constitutes a contract; for example, stock certificates, deeds, bonds, notes.

insured deposits: Deposits that are guaranteed against loss if failure of the financial institution should occur.

insured municipal bond: Municipal bonds that are issued with insurance that covers both principal and interest. The insurance fee is paid by the issuer and these bonds receive high ratings because of the protection against default.

intangible asset: Any asset that has no physical substance, the value of which is hard to measure, such as a patent, trademark, and goodwill.

interest: (1) Part or whole ownership of or right to something of value. (2) The cost of borrowing money. The interest rate is usually expressed as a percentage of the principal amount.

interest rate: Stated as a percentage of principal amount, the charge for the use of money or capital.

interest rate options: Option contracts to buy or sell a specified amount of a particular underlying financial instrument at a specific future date at a predetermined price.

interest rate risk: (1) The risk that interest rates will move above current levels on a locked-in or fixed rate instrument. (2) The risk that longer-term fixed income securities will go down in market value if general interest rates go up. If a security of this type must be liquidated before maturity, the investor may also face capital risk.

Intermarket Trading System (ITS): The electronic system that links the American, Boston, Midwest, New York, Pacific, and Philadelphia stock exchanges. Through this system any market maker or broker of the exchanges can reach another for possible executions of orders.

intermediaries: Financial institutions, such as commercial banks and savings and loan associations, that accept deposits on which they will pay interest and then reinvest those funds in higher yielding securities.

intermediate term: Technical term, generally meaning several weeks to several months. Technical analysts often given recommendations based on an intermediate time frame.

intermediation: The process of intermediaries reinvesting funds placed on deposit into higher yielding securities than the intermediaries are allowed by law to pay their customers. *Compare* disintermediation.

Intermountain Stock Exchange: Address: 39 Exchange Place, Salt Lake City, Utah 84111.

internal financing: Covering cost of expansion through use of retained earnings rather than issuing stocks or bonds.

Internal Revenue Service: The federal agency responsible for the collection of federal income taxes and enforcement of the United States tax laws.

international corporation: A corporation engaged in business in several countries.

international depository receipt: Similar to an American depository receipt. Receipts for certificates of shares in a corporation of a foreign country.

International Monetary Fund: An international financial agency of the United Nations established to maintain orderly world balance of trade and establish currency exchange rates. In 1968 they created Special Drawing Rights (SDRs), commonly called paper gold, to handle member trade debts.

intervals: The established schedule of exercise prices at which new series of options are introduced. The standard intervals are:

Price of Underlying Security	Interval
$50 or less	5 points
$50 to $200	10 points
Over $200	20 points

inter vivos trust: Trust established in which there is a transfer of property from one living person to another.

in-the-money: (1) A call option contract for which the striking (exercise) price of the call is below the market price of the underlying security. (2) A put option contract for which the striking (exercise) price of the put is above the market price of the underlying security.

intrastate securities offering: Offering of securities of companies that operate within one state and sell their securities only to residents of that state.

intrinsic value: (1) The value inherent in something by its very nature. (2) The amount by which a call or put stock option is in-the-money. It is the difference between the current market value of the underlying security and strike (exercise) price of the option.

invested capital: Ownership shares. Funds received for equity capital.

investment: The commitment of funds for the purchase of real assets or securities for the purpose of profit and/or income.

investment advisor: An individual or firm in the business of offering investment guidance or supervision of investment portfolios for a fee. They must abide by SEC and state registration requirements. *Also called* investment counselor.

Investment Advisors Act of 1940: Act requiring registration and reporting of firms and individuals who provide investment advice for a fee.

investment analysis: The study, interpretation, and evaluation of all information available on various investment alternatives to determine risk, projected price movements, and so on, and to suggest appropriate courses of action.

investment banker: The individual or firm who is known as the underwriter and aids a corporation in bringing its securities to the public. In addition to initial and primary offerings the investment banker may also handle large blocks of stock in the secondary market.

investment banking: Process of assisting a corporation in bringing its securities to the market either through public offerings or private placements.

investment clubs: Groups of individuals who pool their money and invest a single amount.

investment company: A company formed for the purpose of selling shares to the public. The proceeds are then invested in other securities according to some predetermined investment plan. There are two types of investment companies, both subject to the Investment Company Act of 1940. One is the open-end investment company which is commonly called a mutual fund and offers new shares on a continuous basis. The other is a closed-end fund which issues only a specified number of shares to the public. These shares are then traded on the open market. *See* closed-end investment company, mutual fund, open-end fund.

Investment Company Act of 1940: Act of Congress that requires registration of and sets regulations for investment companies.

Investment Company Institute: Address: 1775 K Street N.W., Washington, D.C. 20006.

investment grade: (1) Based on fundamental information, this describes an investment situation where the company has a very strong balance sheet, is well capitalized, is a leader in its industry and has a record of continuous dividend payments. (2) A bond rating of Baa/BBB or higher. Bonds designated as investment grade quality are suitable for purchases by fiduciaries.

investment feature: The characteristics and quality of a particular type of investment. The five basic features are: income potential, growth potential, safety of principal, tax advantages, and a balance of features.

investment fund: *See* investment company.

investment manager: One who has the responsibility of investing the funds of institutions or individuals.

investment objective: The personal financial goals of an investor, for example, income or growth based on considerations such as age, marital status, dependents, income, and personal temperament.

investor: One who commits funds to real assets or securities for the purpose of receiving a profit and/or income.

IRA: *See* individual retirement account.

irredeemable bond: *See* annuity bond.

issue: (1) Placing a new offering of securities on the market. (2) Securities that have been sold or are to be sold to the public.

issued capital stock: All authorized capital shares of a corporation that have at any time been issued to the public or exchanged for goods and services.

issue price: The price at which a security offering will be sold to the public.

issuer: (1) The corporation that is offering or has offered bonds, notes, or stock for public sale or private placement. (2) For listed option contract, the Options Clearing Corporation is the issuer.

jargon: Terms used with special meanings in a particular field of business or activity.

joint account: An account held by two or more parties. Each party shares in the liabilities, privileges, and profits inherent in the account.

joint bond: *See* guaranteed bond.

joint endorsement: Signatures required on an instrument by two or more parties due to the fact that the instrument is made payable to those individuals.

joint stock company: A rare form of business organization that issues stocks, but carries with it unlimited liability for the shareholders.

joint tenants account (as tenants in common): An account in which cash and/or securities are jointly owned by two or more parties. Each party shares equally in the liabilities and profits of the account. Upon the death of any one tenant, his or her interest passes to their estate and not to the surviving tenants.

joint tenants account (with rights of survivorship): An account in which cash and/or securities are jointly owned by two or more parties. Each shares equally in the liabilities and profits of the account. Upon the death of any one tenant, their interest passes to the surviving tenants without becoming part of the deceased's estate.

joint venture: A general term used to indicate two or more parties joined together in a business venture in order to receive income or profit.

junior bond: Bond that is subordinate to other debt instruments in event of claims upon the assets of the issuer.

junior equity: Common stock. In event of distribution or liquidation, common stock takes a junior position to other equity and debt securities.

karat: A unit used to measure the content of gold. One karat equals 1/24 proportion of pure gold. *Compare* carat.

Karat Count	Purity
24	100 percent gold
22	91 percent gold
18	75 percent gold
14	58 percent gold
10	41 percent gold

Keogh plan: A tax-favored, self-funded retirement plan that enables self-employed individuals to contribute to tax-deferred retirement plans. The current allowance is the lesser of $15,000 or 15 percent of earned income. *See* individual retirement account.

Keynesian Economic Theory: An economic theory attributed to John Maynard Keynes. Under this theory, it is believed that economic growth and income are influenced by investment capital and the multiplier effect of such investments.

killing: To make extraordinary profits in the stock market due to a combination of carefully chosen investments, good timing, and luck.

know your customer rule: New York Stock Exchange rule requiring that the broker learn all essential facts relative to the clients and the nature of the accounts before approving the opening of a brokerage account.

labor intense industry: An industry that requires a large number of employed individuals in relation to the total capital investment. *Compare* capital intense industry.

lagging indicators: Economic indicators that show a major change after other indicators of economic activity have already changed direction. *Compare* coincident indicators, leading indicators.

lamb: An inexperienced, unsophisticated investor with little knowledge of the investment world.

last-in, first-out (LIFO): Inventory evaluation method that assumes for tax and accounting purposes that the last materials purchased are the first to be sold or used for further production. *Compare* first-in, first-out.

late tape: Term used when the announcement of trades and their prices on a particular exchange lags behind trading activity.

leaders: Those securities that move—either up or down—ahead of the general market.

leading indicators: Economic indicators that show a major change before other indicators of economic activity have significantly moved. *Compare* coincident indicators, lagging indicators.

ledger debit balance: The amount of money that a client owes to his brokerage firm for transactions, commissions, interest, and other fees.

leg: One side of a straddle option position.

legal list: Investment alternatives on a state approved list that are thought to be appropriate for investments by fiduciaries and regulated companies such as banks, insurance companies and other financial institutions. *Also called* legal investments.

legal opinion: Statement by legal counsel that a municipal bond offering has been issued in accordance with the present laws of the municipality and that the interest is or is not exempt from federal, state or local taxation. The legal opinion is considered necessary for good delivery.

lending agreement: Document signed by the investor with a margin account that authorizes the brokerage firm to lend margined securities held in the account.

letter of intent: Document signed by mutual fund buyers stating that they plan, over a 13-month period, to buy sufficient shares of the fund to qualify for a reduced sales charge.

letter stock: Unregistered common stock privately issued by corporations to certain key individuals. The shares cannot be resold on the open market and can only be transferred by private sale.

level charge plans: Mutual fund plans used for acquiring additional shares over a period of time. The sales charge is made each time additional shares are purchased and is based on the dollar amount of the investment.

leverage: (1) The use of debt capital for expansion to increase return on equity. The amount of leverage capital has a definite impact on market price of common stock. If a large debt must be serviced and earnings are low, market price will often come down. (2) The use of margin or borrowed money to buy securities to improve percentage gain.

leverage fund: A mutual fund that is allowed by its charter to borrow money to increase the quantity of securities it may purchase with the aim of increasing its return.

liabilities: Claims against the assets of a corporation or individuals. Something that is owed.

LIFO: *See* last-in, first-out.

lift a leg: To close out one side of an option straddle, while leaving the other side open. *See* leg, straddle.

limited liability: A feature of corporations and some partnerships in which shareholders or partners are liable only up to the value of their investment.

limited partnership: A partnership form of business in which certain partners are liable only to the extent of their investment. These partners usually do not participate in the management of the business. One or more other partners would be fully liable for the debts of the business.

limited tax bond: A debt instrument issued by a municipality based on the ad valorem value of real estate within a certain taxing area.

limited trading authorization: Approval for someone other than the brokerage client to have trading privileges in the account of the client. This authorization is limited to purchase and sales.

limit move: The highest or lowest price an exchange will allow a futures contract to move during a single trading day before it closes trading on that contract. The purpose of this action is to stabilize the market.

limit order: A buy or sell order for a stated number of shares of a specific security placed at a specified price. The order is to be executed at the specified (limit) price or better. Typically, the buy limit order is placed below current market price and states the maximum purchase price. The sell limit order is placed above the current market price and sets the minimum sale price. When the limit is not within the current quote, the order is said to be "away from the market."

limit-or-market-on-close order: An order to buy or sell a stated number of shares of a specific security at a limit (specified) price. If the order cannot be executed as a limit order, then it is to be executed as a market order at or as near to the close of trading as possible.

line chart: A price-time axis chart that depicts price changes over a period of time by a single line connecting the prices.

liquid: (1) Having sufficient cash or cash equivalents to meet short-term financial obligations. (2) An asset or other investment that can easily be converted into cash. *Compare* illiquid.

liquid assets: Those assets of a corporation that include cash and items easily converted into cash.

liquidation: (1) To dissolve a business by selling all assets, paying outstanding obligations, and distributing the remainder to shareholders. (2) In an investment account, liquidation means to close out positions an investor is holding for cash.

liquidity: (1) Investors' ability to convert securities into cash on short notice with minimal or no loss in current market value. (2) The ability of the market system to handle significant increases in the trading volume of a security with only minor price adjustments. (3) Corporate ability to meet obligations out of liquid assets.

listed option contracts: Stock option contracts, issued by the OCC, that are traded in an organized auction market on the floor of a member exchange. The striking prices and expiration dates are set in advance, and adjustments are made in the event of a stock split or stock dividend. Listed options trade in a liquid market, which allows the buyers and sellers to close out their positions at any time or to exercise their contracts at will. *Compare* unlisted option.

listed securities: Those securities that have been accepted for trading by a registered exchange.

listing: Meeting requirements and receiving acceptance by an exchange for trading.

little man: *See* small investor.

LMV: *See* long market value.

load: *See* load charge.

load charge: This is a sales charge on some mutual funds, made at the time the investor purchases shares in the fund, and covers commissions and other expenses. These charges can vary from six to eight percent, depending on the type of fund. *Also called* front-end load, load.

load spread option: Method of payment for the sales charge of mutual funds issued on a contractual plan basis.

loaned stock: Stock loaned to a short-seller by the brokerage firm, in order to cover delivery to the buyer of those shares.

loan value: The amount a brokerage firm may loan client for margined purchases of securities.

local bill: Term used to describe the printed confirmations of transactions that are prepared and mailed to investors for their trades and open orders.

locked-in: Situation where an investor cannot sell securities that he owns or shift his investment dollars because the profit received would adversely affect his tax situation.

locked-out: Being in a position where the investor cannot take advantage of investment situations because of market conditions.

long: Term used to describe ownership of securities. For example, if an investor is long 500 shares of ABC Corporation, this would mean he owns 500 shares of ABC Corporation. *Compare* short/short sale.

long call: A call option contract that has been purchased on an opening purchase transaction. *Compare* short call.

long market value (LMV): LMV is the current market value calculated on a daily basis of the long securities held in a brokerage account. *Compare* short market value.

long option position: A stock option contract that has been purchased on an opening purchase transaction.

long put: A put option contract that has been purchased on an opening purchase transaction. *Compare* short put.

long sale: The sale of securities that a customer owns. *Compare* short/short sale.

long term: (1) More than one year. (2) One complete Bull/Bear cycle.

long-term capital gains: Profits on investments held more than one year.

long-term capital losses: Losses on investments held more than one year.

long-term liability: A debt obligation that will come due in more than one year. Generally speaking, long-term debts are those due in ten or more years.

long-term investment: A security investment made with the intention of holding it more than one year, usually for a relatively long period of time. In such an investment one looks for growth in value or income rather than short-term profits.

losses: (1) The difference between the amount invested and the amount recovered when the amount invested is greater than what is realized upon liquidation. (2) The difference between all income and expense when income is less than expense.

low: Used in retrospect to indicate the lowest price a security or market indicator reached during any given time period.

low grade: In rating securities, this indicates an uncertainty of the issuer's ability to meet financial obligaions, management strength, and its position in its industry.

M 1: A calculation of the nation's money supply using the total of all curren-

cy held by the public plus demand deposits.

M 2: A broader calculation of the nation's money supply using the total of all currency, demand deposits, commercial bank time deposits, money-market mutual fund deposits, and overnight repurchase agreements.

M 3: A broader calculation of the nation's money supply using the total of all currency, demand deposits, commercial bank time deposits, money-market mutual fund deposits, overnight repurchase agreements, savings held by savings institutions, larger time deposits, and longer term repurchase agreements.

macroeconomics: The study of the nation's economy or other economic units as a whole rather than its individual parts. *Compare* microeconomics.

maintenance call: The demand upon the brokerage client to deposit funds in his margin account in order to bring it up to the minimum maintenance margin requirement.

maintenance excess: The dollar amount by which a client's equity exceeds minimum maintenance requirements in a margin account.

maintenance fee: A fee charged by some mutual funds that is deducted quarterly to pay for the reinvestment of dividends and capital gains.

maintenance margin requirement: The minimum margin that must be maintained in margin accounts based on the long or short market value of securities held in the account and determined at the close of each business day. If the long or short market value of securities moves below this requirement, a maintenance call is issued to the customer.

major bottom: An anticipated situation in which it is believed that market prices have reached their lowest values.

majority stockholder: A party owning sufficient shares in a corporation to have effective or working control.

make a market: To maintain an inventory of certain shares of stock for resale to the public and to attempt to smooth possible volatile price fluctuations. Dealers make a market in over-the-counter securities and specialists make a market in listed securities.

management company: A company in the business of managing financial investments for others by supervising investment portfolios.

management fee: A fee charged by investment companies for their services.

manager's fee: A fee imposed on the issuer by the underwriters in a public offering or private placement.

manipulation: Illegal practice of creating artificial trading activity in a stock in order to raise or lower the market price to induce others to buy or sell.

margin: Investor's equity in securities purchased in a margin account. For example, on a security purchase amounting to $10,000, if the client pays $6,000 on the purchase, 60 percent has been margined and the other 40 percent has been borrowed from the brokerage firm.

marginable securities: Securities that have been approved for purchase on a margin basis.

margin account: A brokerage account that allows the investor to buy or sell securities on credit within the rules of the Federal Reserve and the exchanges.

margin agreement: A document signed by the client to open a margin account in which he agrees to abide by certain regulations and permits the brokerage firm to have a lien on the account. *Also called* hypothecation agreement.

margin call: A demand upon the client for a deposit of additional cash or securities to meet initial margin requirements. The call is made when a long or short position is created in the margin account. If sufficient equity is in the account, it will be used in place of requesting additional cash or securities.

margined securities: Securities that have been hypothecated and purchased in a margin account.

margin minimum requirement: Stated as a percentage of the total value of securities being purchased, this is the minimum dollar amount of cash or value of marginable securities an investor must place on deposit to buy additional securities on margin. Margin requirements are set by the Federal Reserve Board.

mark down: The amount subtracted from the actual price by a dealer to arrive at the selling price. For example, in selling securities through the over-the-counter market, instead of charging a commission the dealer may take a dealer's mark down from the actual price. *Compare* mark up.

marked to the market: The demand to deposit additional funds to make up the difference between current market value of a security and the value of the contract it is securing under a security loan agreement if the market price of the stock changes.

market: (1) The place where buyers and sellers come together to publicly trade—the stock exchanges. (2) The process of buyers and sellers coming together to trade. (3) The highest bid and lowest offer at any given time for a security. (4) The supply and demand for a given item or security. (5) The availability of shares of any given security. (6) To promote a product or security.

marketable securities: A security that is easily converted into cash with minimal or no loss in current market value.

market analysis: The study of factors affecting supply and demand relationships, investor psychology, monetary factors, and price and volume movements of market indicators, and of individual securities in order to determine the probable direction and extent of future price movements.

market average: Term often used to indicate the Dow Jones Industrial Average. Market averages are approximate arithmetic means used to measure prices of securities within some set group. This average is then used as a guide to the movement of the markets as a whole.

market bottom: The lowest point that a market indicator reaches for a given period of time. A bottom must, therefore, be followed by some degree of recovery.

market breadth: (1) The number of shares of any given security that are publicly traded. (2) The scope and strength of the market direction. Breadth is measured by several indicators including advance/decline figures and volume momentum.

market index: Any one of the various indexes that gives information on market prices and volume.

market letter: A publication giving information on the securities markets and/or recommendations on individual securities. These market letters are prepared by brokerage firms and advisory services for general distribution to their clients.

market maker: A dealer or specialist that buys and sells certain securities to and/or from investors from their own accounts. Through this inventory of shares, the market maker attempts to stabilize volatile price fluctuations by buying and selling from his own account to narrow the spread between bid and asked prices and to make the market more liquid.

market-on-the-close order: A market order to buy or sell securities that requires execution at the close of trad-

ing for that day, or as near to it as possible.

market-on-the-opening order: A market order to buy or sell securities that requires execution on the opening of trading for that day.

market opening: The initial opening transactions on a particular exchange. The New York Stock Exchange and American Stock Exchange open at 10:00 a.m. Eastern time for trading. Most of the securities listed will then open and begin trading.

market order: A buy or sell order for a stated number of shares of a particular security placed "at the market." The order is to be executed at the best possible price at the time it reaches the post or desk at which the stock is traded. Compare limit order.

market price: (1) The highest bid and lowest offer. (2) The actual trading price of the last transaction for a particular security. Market price may change from one transaction to the next.

market risk: The risk involved in owning securities that the market value will move up or down with no control on the part of the investor.

market top: The highest point that a market indicator reaches for a given period of time. A top must therefore be followed by some degree of decline.

market trend: The general prevailing direction—either up or down—of the markets as a whole.

market volume: The number of shares traded on a given exchange in a single day or the number of shares traded for one security in a given day.

mark up: The amount added to the actual price by a dealer to arrive at the purchase price. Compare mark down.

married put: A stock put option and shares of the underlying security purchased on the same day and identified as such.

Massachusetts trust: A corporate business form that is organized as a trust and that has a board of trustees instead of a board of directors. Transferable shares are issued and shareholders have limited liability.

matched and lost: A situation that occurs when two offers (or two bids) of equal size and price to sell (or buy) the same security reach the floor simultaneously. A coin is flipped to determine which order will be filled first.

matched orders: An illegal manipulative practice where individuals buy through one brokerage house and sell through another to create the illusion of heavy volume in a particular security.

maturity: The date on which a financial obligation becomes due and must be redeemed by the issuing corporation.

MBIA: *See* Municipal Bond Insurance Association.

measuring gap: A price gap that duplicates the most recent move. *See* gap.

medium term: *See* intermediate term.

member: Person, firm, or corporation who has applied for and received membership on an exchange. They must agree to abide by the rules of the exchange, pass an examination and pay an initiation fee. (Note: On the NYSE only real people may obtain seats and be members and those members may not be associated with more than one member firm or corporation.)

member bank: A bank that has been admitted to the Federal Reserve System.

member corporation: A corporation, registered as a broker or dealer, that has at least one partner or employee who is a member on a securities exchange.

members' short sale ratio: Calculated by dividing all shares sold short by members for their own accounts by total short sales for the same period. It indicates a negative sentiment when member short selling is 85 percent or more and positive when the ratio is 68 percent or less.

merger: The purchase of all assets of one corporation by another corporation. The merged firm may or may not continue to operate under its own name and management.

MGIC Indemnity Corporation: A subsidiary of MGIC Investment Corporation that offers insurance on certain municipal bonds.

MGIC Investment Corporation: A holding company that, through its subsidiaries, offers insurance on residential and commercial mortgages, commercial leases, and certain municipal bonds.

microeconomics: The study of the individual parts of the economy and other economic units. *Compare* macroeconomics.

Mid-America Commodity Exchange: Address: 175 West Jackson Blvd., Chicago, Illinois 60604.

Midwest Stock Exchange: Address: 120 South LaSalle Street, Chicago, Illinois 60603.

mill: One mill is equal to one percent or .001 and commonly used in setting rates for property taxes.

Minneapolis Grain Exchange: Address: 400 South Fourth Street, Minneapolis, Minnesota 55475.

minority interest: Ownership in a corporation in which those shares allow no effective or working control.

minus tick: A transaction that occurs at a lower price than the previous transaction.

minus yield: Situation where a convertible bond is selling at a premium that is greater than the interest yield on the bond.

MIP: *See* monthly investment plan.

missing the market: A limit order that is not filled because the market price of the security moved away from the limit price set for the order.

modified legal list: Investment guidelines used in certain states that allow fiduciaries to invest the majority of funds in legal list securities and a portion in other securities not on that list.

momentum: Meausrement of the strength and pace of trends in individual stocks, industry groups, and market indicators.

momentum indicators: Market indicators (usually expressed as moving averages) that use price and volume figures to determine the strength or weakness of the current market and any overbought or oversold conditions, and to identify turning points in the markets.

monetary indicators: Indicators designed to study the actions and policies of the Federal Reserve and Treasury Department that could have an effect on equity and bond markets. They measure the liquidity available in the economy that can be added to the markets, and they measure yield relations between alternative investments.

monetary policy: Policies implemented by the Federal Reserve Board to increase or decrease the supply of money and credit.

money: A generally accepted medium of exchange having a specific stated value.

money market: The international dealer market of trading short-term financial instruments (typically with maturities of one year or less) issued by governments, corporations and financial institutions. The principal money market securities are Treasury bills, commercial paper, banker's accept-

ance, and negotiable certificates of deposit. *Compare* capital markets.

money market fund: A mutual fund that trades in short-term money market instruments. Most money market funds are no-load and money can be withdrawn with one day notice and no penalty.

money market instruments: Short-term financial instruments with maturities of one year or less that trade in the international money markets. Principal money market securities are Treasury Bills, Commercial Paper, Banker's Acceptance, and Negotiable Certificates of Deposit. There is an active primary and secondary market available.

money spread: *See* calendar spread, vertical spread.

money supply: The amount of a nation's currency in circulation, demand deposits, and other deposits. Increasing or decreasing the supply of money is a key tool of the Federal Reserve Board in controlling economic conditions. *See* M 1, M 2, M 3.

money supply indicator: Percentage change in the money supply adjusted for the percentage change in the Consumer Price Index. When the money supply is increasing at a fairly steady rate and inflation is low, stock prices tend to rise. When there is a contraction of money supply growth or an increase in the rate of inflation, it is considered an unfavorable development for the stock markets.

monthly investment plan: A New York Stock Exchange sponsored program that permits small investors to purchase stock at a minimum dollar amount monthly or quarterly. This is similar to a dollar-cost-averaging method of investing.

Montreal Stock Exchange: Address: The Stock Exchange Tower, 800 Victoria Square, Montreal, Quebec, Canada H42 1A9.

Moody's Investors Service: An independent service that reviews, compares, and provides ratings for securities, while also furnishing other financial information to investors.

moral obligation bonds: Revenue-backed municipal bonds issued by an agency of the state. Though they are not general obligations bonds, it is assumed that, in the event of default, the state will provide funds to cover both principal and interest.

mortgage: Pledging property as security for the payment of a debt.

mortgage bond: A bond that is backed by specific property of the issuing corporation.

mortgage-participation certificate: A pass-through security that represents an undivided interest in a pool of mortgages that the Federal Home Loan Mortgage Corporation has purchased. The mortgages are packaged and resold through these certificates. *See* Federal Home Loan Mortgage Corporation.

moving average: Average prices that are continually updated for a specified period of time. The average is calculated daily and as a new current price is added, the oldest price is deleted from the average. This method smoothes out short-term movements and therefore more accurately represents true values.

multiplier effect: The theory that a relatively minor event can cause a great change in another area. For example, when an investment is made for expansion of a plant, this will create additional jobs, which will increase retail spending and savings, and also affect other economic areas.

muni: Term widely used for municipal bonds.

municipal bond: A bond issued by a government authority such as a state, county, city or governmental subdivision other than the federal goverment. The interest received is generally free from federal, state, and local income taxes. Municipal bonds fall into four main categories: general obligation, revenue, industrial revenue, and public housing authority.

Municipal Bond Insurance Association (MBIA): A pool of insurance companies that insure the payment of both interest and principal on certain municipal bonds at maturity. All municipal bonds with MBIA insurance are rated AAA.

municipal notes: Short-term securities of several months up to several years issued by a municipal authority.

Municipal Securities Rulemaking Board: The self-regulating board that establishes the rules and registration requirements for the municipal securities industry.

Munifacts: A subscription service that provides information about new municipal bond offerings.

mutual fund: An investment company subject to the regulations of the Investment Company Act of 1940, which pools funds of individuals and invests those funds on the investors' behalf. New shares are continuously sold by the fund and shares outstanding will be redeemed by the fund at the investor's request. *Also called* open-end investment company. *See* open-end investment company. *Compare* closed-end investment company.

mutual fund cash ratio: The percentage of mutual funds' cash in relation to their total assets. Ten percent or higher is thought to be positive and six percent or below is considered unfavorable. A high ratio of cash to total assets is considered bullish because funds are available for investment. But an increasing cash percentage is bearish beacuse it shows that mutual funds are withdrawing from the market.

naked: *See* uncovered.

naked option: A short stock option position for which the writer (seller) does not hold a hedged position in the underlying security. *See* uncovered option.

naked option writer: *See* uncovered writer.

narrow market: Security trading with a minor spread between the bid and asked prices. *Also called* narrow spread.

NASD: *See* National Association of Securities Dealers.

NASDAQ: *See* National Association of Securities Dealers Automatic Quotation.

NASDAQ indexes: The NASDAQ indexes include trading price averages computed by using over 3,000 domestic over-the-counter companies. The seven NASDAQ indexes are the industrials, banks, insurance companies, other financial institutions, transportations, utilities, and the composite.

NASD 5 percent policy: A nonrigid rule for NASD members that suggests that commissions and markups and markdowns be about five percent on a typical transaction, but in all cases be fair. Exceptions to this five percent rule include mutual fund sales, small transactions, transactions that are difficult to complete, and exempt securities.

NASD Rules of Fair Practice: NASD rules that establish the ethics for the securities industry to ensure fair and just dealings between members and their clients.

National Association of Investment Clubs: Address: 1515 East Eleven Mile Road, Royal Oak, Michigan 48067.

National Association of Securities Dealers (NASD): Self-regulating trade association of brokers and dealers involved in the over-the-counter securities business. The SEC has granted the NASD certain powers to administer and enforce self-regulating policies. Address: 1735 K Street N.W., Washington, D.C. 20006.

National Association of Securities Dealers Automatic Quotation (NASDAQ): A securities quotation system for reporting trades on over 3,000 domestic over-the-counter securities. The NASDAQ issues four or five identifying symbols for the various securities. Three levels of subscription service are available. Level one is for member firm offices. Level two is intended for institutional and certain retail traders. Level three is to provide market makers a system to enter their firm bid and asked prices.

National Daily Quotation Service: Quotation service of the National Quotation Bureau. *See* National Quotation Bureau.

National Income: The total income earned for the nation's final goods and services. *See* gross national product.

National Quotation Bureau: The organization that issues quotations on over-the-counter securities. *See* pink sheets, white sheets, yellow sheets.

National Securities Clearing Corporation: Independent clearing organization used to execute and settle transactions between member firms. Address: 55 Water Street, New York, New York 10041.

National Securities Exchange: Any exchange registered with the SEC. However, the term "regional exchange" is commonly used to identify an exchange located outside of New York City. The following are exchanges registered with the Securities and Exchange Commission:
American Stock Exchange
Boston Stock Exchange
Chicago Board Options Exchange
Chicago Board of Trade
Cincinnati Stock Exchange
Intermountain Stock Exchange
Midwest Stock Exchange
New York Stock Exchange
Pacific Stock Exchange
Philadelphia Stock Exchange
Spokane Stock Exchange
The Honolulu Stock Exchange has been exempt from registration.

National Securities Trade Association: An organization of brokers and dealers involved in the over-the-counter markets. Address: 55 Broad Street, New York, New York 10004.

NAV: *See* net asset value.

near option: That side of a stock spread option position that expires before the other side does. *See* spread. *Compare* far option.

near term: Technical research evaluation of market performance that usually indicates a one- to five-week time period.

negotiable certificate of deposit (CD): Negotiable money market instrument issued by banks usually for $100,000 or more that has a negotiated rate. These instruments trade on the open market and offer the investor an excellent return and high degree of safety. *See* certificate of deposit. *Compare* nonnegotiable certificate of deposit.

negotiable instrument: Any legal instrument, such as a stock certificate, that may be sold or transferred by endorsement and delivery, or only delivery in cases where the instrument is not registered.

negotiable order of withdrawal account (NOW): An interest-bearing account offered by commercial banks, savings and loan associations, and other financial institutions that may also serve as a checking account. The holders can withdraw funds from their accounts by means of a check.

net asset value: Mutual fund book value per share. The total assets minus total liabilities divided by the total number of shares outstanding. Mutual fund shares are typically sold at net asset value plus a sales charge and are repurchased by the fund at net asset value.

net change: The change in the price of a security from the close of one trading day to the close of the next trading day.

net income: The profit remaining after all deductions for operations, taxes, interest, and reserves. Often called earnings, or earnings per share.

net investment income: The profit realized on an investment less all commissions and other fees and expenses.

net position: The net of an investor's short positions and his long positions. The investor would either hold a net long or net short position.

net profit: Earnings after all operation costs and debt service have been taken into account. The figure is sometimes used before federal taxes have been paid, but most often it is quoted as an after-tax profit.

net spendable income: *See* discretionary income.

net unrealized appreciation: The appreciation between investment cost and current market value of an individual's holdings.

net unrealized depreciation: The decline between investment cost and the current market value of an individual's holdings.

net volume: The difference between uptick volume and downtick volume.

net worth: (1) The net difference between total assets and total liabilities. (2) The equity ownership of a business, shareholders' interest, or partnership interest.

neutral trend: A security's prevailing price direction is sideways.

new high: The highest price a security or market index has ever reached. However, the term is most often used to indicate a new high for a given time period.

new highs: The number of issues that on any given trading day have reached their highest price for the past year.

new issue: A bond or stock issue that is being offered for public sale for the first time.

new low: The lowest price a security or market index has ever reached. However, the term is most often used to indicate a new low for a given time period.

new lows: The number of issues that on any given trading day have reached their lowest price for the past year.

news ticker: Device found in brokerage offices that gives up-to-the-minute news stories about important corporate developments, economic conditions, and market information. *Also called* news wire.

New York call money: The term used to describe money borrowed by brokerage firms to meet short-term financial needs due to credit extended to their clients who maintain margin accounts. *See* brokers' loan rate.

New York Cocoa Exchange: Address: 127 John Street, New York, New York 10038.

New York Coffee and Sugar Exchange: Address: 4 World Trade Center, New York, New York 10048.

New York Cotton Exchange: Address: 4 World Trade Center, New York, New York 10048.

New York Curb Exchange: The former name of the American Stock Exchange.

New York Futures Exchange: A subsidiary of the New York Stock Exchange that handles trading of financial futures contracts.

New York Mercantile Exchange: Address: 4 World Trade Center, New York, New York 10048.

New York plan: A method of transferring ownership of equipment purchased through the use of equipment trust certificates, in which the title to the equipment passes to the purchaser as the debt is retired. *Compare* Philadelphia plan. *See* equipment trust certificates.

New York Stock Exchange: Often called the Exchange or Big Board and abbreviated to NYSE. The New York Stock Exchange is the largest securities exchange in the United States. Address: 11 Wall Street, New York, New York 10005.

New York Stock Exchange Common Stock Index: *See* New York Stock Exchange Composite Index.

New York Stock Exchange Composite Index: Average computed using all of the common shares of companies listed on the NYSE (approximately 1,500 companies). This composite index uses a base-weighted aggregative method to calculate its average. There are four subgroup indexes: NYSE Industrials, NYSE Transportations, NYSE Utilities, and NYSE Financial.

New York Stock Exchange volume: The total of all shares traded for any given trading day on the New York Stock Exchange.

NH: *See* not held order.

nine-bond rule: A NYSE rule that requires any order received by a member firm for nine or less bonds that are listed on the NYSE to first be sent to the floor of the exchange; then if the order cannot be filled in one hour, it may be filled in the over-the-counter market.

no load: No sales charge. In the case of mutual funds, this means the shares are sold at net asset value.

no-load fund: A mutual fund that does not charge its investors a sales charge for investment. The shares are purchased at net asset value.

noncallable bonds: Bonds that are issued with stipulation that they may not be redeemed (called-in) prior to maturity.

noncumulative dividends: Term is usually used in connection with preferred stock. If a dividend is not paid out by a corporation at the normal payment date, it does not accrue for the benefit of the shareholders and is lost forever.

noncumulative preferred stock: Preferred stock that is issued with the stipulation that if a dividend is not paid out by the corporation it does not accrue for the benefit of the preferred shareholders.

noncumulative voting: *See* statutory voting.

noninterest bearing bond: A bond or note issued at a discount. Interest is not earned during the life of the bond or note, but the instrument is redeemed at maturity for full face value. U.S. Treasury bills are issued in this manner.

nonmember bank: A bank that is not a member of the Federal Reserve System.

nonmember firm: A securities firm that is not a member of a particular securities exchange. For example, a firm may be a member of the Philadelphia Exchange but not a member of the New York Stock Exchange.

nonnegotiable certificate of deposit: Nonnegotiable instrument issued by banks and other financial institutions to individuals. These offer an excellent return and high degree of safety but are not negotiable and carry high penalties for early withdrawal.

nonnegotiable instrument: A legal instrument of value that may not be freely or easily sold or transferred to another party.

nonprofit organization: A business chartered to be not-for-profit. It is illegal for any officer, shareholders, or other person to receive a profit from operations. The organization normally maintains a total or partial tax-exempt status.

nontaxable dividend: Money paid to shareholders that is specified as return of capital. While it is a nontaxable event at the time of distribution, the cost basis of the security must be reduced by the amount received.

nonvoting stock: Stock issued by a corporation without voting privileges.

no-par-value stock: Stock issued without a stated par value. On the corporate books a value is assigned by the Board of Directors.

note: (1) A legal instrument that shows evidence of a debt and the maker's promise to pay a specific sum either upon demand or within a specified period of time. Also included on the note are any interest charges or other fees and duties. (2) An unsecured short-term debt obligation generally maturing in seven years or less.

not-held order (NH): A market or limit order with trading instructions that give the floor broker discretion as to the time and price at which the order may be filled. The client agrees in this case not to hold the specialist responsible if the order cannot be filled within the time period required.

not rated (NR): Indication that a security has not been rated by a recognized rating service. The NR has no implied indication of quality or lack of quality.

NOW account: *See* negotiable-order-of-withdrawal-account.

NSTA: *See* National Securities Trade Association.

NYSE: *See* New York Stock Exchange.

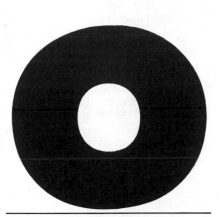

objectives: (1) The investment goals that individual or institutional investors hope to achieve by their investment plans. (2) The price an investor expects a given security will reach during a given time period.

obligation: A legally enforceable debt of either money or duty that one owes to another.

obsolete securities: Securities for which there is no longer a market. In most cases, these may be written off as a loss.

OCC: *See* Options Clearing Corporation.

OCC prospectus: A formal disclosure statement, required by the Securites and Exchange Commission, that must be given to all options clients before they are approved for trading stock option contracts.

odd lot: Any number of shares less than the standard unit of trading. Typically 1 to 99 shares of stock is considered an odd lot.

odd-lot buy/sell ratio: Odd-lot buying divided by odd-lot selling. This ratio is an indicator of sentiment toward the market by odd-lot investors.

odd-lot dealer: Member of the exchange who acts as a dealer (rather than broker) and buys and sells odd-lots of stock to and from other members of an exchange.

odd-lot differential: An extra cost that may be charged to the client to execute an odd-lot transaction. This differential charge is usually one eighth of a point.

odd-lot index: A composite index of odd lot purchases used to determine the investment attitudes of the smaller investor.

odd-lot short sales: A composite index of odd-lot sales used to determine the investment attitudes of the smaller investor.

odd-lot short sales ratio: Odd-lot shares shorted divided by all other odd-lot sales. When the ratio exceeds or reaches 3 percent the indicator is considered positive and when the ratio declines to 0.7 percent or less it is considered negative.

odd-lot theory: A theory that states investors who purchase odd-lot quantities of securities are usually late in timing of their investments. They wait until a move has already been made, therefore the sophisticated investor should move in the opposite direction of the odd-lot investor. However, data has shown that at almost every major market bottom, odd-lot investors have been buyers rather than sellers. And, at almost every major market top, there is a lower buy-to-sell ratio.

odd-lot trend: Indicator used to compare odd-lot buying volume to odd-lot selling volume. It is believed by some that high odd-lot buying typically will indicate a downturn and high odd-lot selling will indicate an upturn in the market.

offer: (1) To present, propose, or tender. (2) To present for sale. (3) The price at which an individual is willing to sell. It is the asked price for a security.

offering: A security issue (stocks, bonds, or notes) being offered for sale to the public.

offering circular: The prospectus that must be made available to any potential investor during an initial security offering. It includes complete information regarding the company, its officers, its financial status, and the proposed use of the funds to be received from the offering.

offering price: (1) The price at which a security will be sold to the public in an offering. (2) The asked price of a security. (3) The price an investor would pay for one share when investing in a mutual fund. It amounts to the net asset value with the sales charge added if there is one.

officer: A member of corporate management that may within certain legal limits act for the corporation. Usually included are the president, secretary, treasurer, and certain key employees.

official statement: Similar to an offering circular. The statement gives the details of a new municipal bond offering.

off-the-board: A trade that takes place without being executed on an exchange. This includes over-the-counter transactions and special situations, such as trades through the fourth market.

on balance volume: A cumulative net of up-volume and down-volume. Higher volume on price increases is generally considered positive; higher volume on price declines is generally considered negative.

open: *See* opening.

open-end fund: *See* open-end investment company.

open-end investment company: An investment company, subject to the regulations of the Investment Company Act of 1940, that continuously issues new shares to the public. The proceeds received are then invested in other securities according to some predetermined plan. By regulation, at least 90 percent of the income and capital gains must be distributed to shareholders in order to remain nontaxable to the fund. Upon demand by the shareholders, the open-end investment company must redeem or repurchase the shares. By contrast the closed-end investment company issues only a specified number of shares to the public; which then trade on the open market. *Also called* mutual fund. *See* investment company. *Compare* closed-end investment company.

open-end investment trust: *See* open-end investment company.

open-end mutual fund: A mutual fund that continuously offers new shares for public sales. *See* open-end investment company.

opening: The first transaction for a given security on any particular trading day.

opening block: The first transaction of a trading session for a particular security. It may appear as a single block transaction, but is typically an accumulation of a number of individual orders.

opening price: For any given security, it is the price at which the first transaction of the day is executed. This may be the same or different than the previous trading day's closing price.

opening purchase transaction: An option transaction in which the option client becomes the holder (buyer) of an option contract; giving the holder the right to buy or sell shares on the underlying security.

opening rotation: The trading rotation in which an effort is made to establish an initial price level where buy and sell

O

orders will be in balance in respect to both volume and price.

opening sale transaction: An option transaction in which the option client becomes the writer (seller) of an option contract; giving the writer the obligation to buy or sell shares on the underlying security.

opening transaction: The purchase or sale of an option contract that creates an open position and gives the right or obligation to buy or sell shares on the underlying stock.

open interest: The number of outstanding option contracts that have been issued on an underlying stock of the same class and series that have not been closed out, have not been exercised and have not expired.

open market: A market available to all potential buyers and sellers, such as the securities markets.

open market operation: The Federal Reserve activity of buying and selling government sercurities on the open market as a means of expanding or contracting the credit supply.

open option: *See* outstanding option.

open order: Any order that has not yet been executed to buy or sell securities either for the day or until canceled.

OPG: A security trading designation (derived from the word "opening") that requires that a buy or sell order is to be executed at the market price at the opening of trading (or at a specific limit price when a limit order is placed), any portion not executed is automatically canceled.

opportunity cost: The benefits given up by choosing one investment alternative over another. For example, if one invests in high yielding stocks he might be giving up a high rate of growth on another investment.

option: A contractual agreement between the holder (buyer) and the writer (seller) to purchase or sell shares of the underlying security in 100-share lots at a specific price within a predetermined period of time. *See* call option contact, put option contract, stock option.

option account agreement form: A special brokerage account form that must be filled out and signed by all option clients, disclosing their financial status and prior investment experience. In addition, they agree to abide by the Options Clearing Corporation and exchange rules.

optional bond: A bond that is issued with the stipulation that it may be called in by the issuing corporation prior to maturity and/or redeemed by the holder prior to maturity date.

optional dividend: A dividend in which the shareholder may choose to take cash or additional shares or a combination of cash and shares of stocks.

option contract: The agreement that exists between the writer and holder of an exchange traded option that has been issued by the OCC.

option order: An order directed to a national exchange through a clearing member to establish (open) or terminate (close) an option contract. The option order must specify (1) whether it is a buy or sell, (2) whether it is to open or close a position, (3) the number of contracts involved, (4) the type of option—whether it is a put or call, (5) the name of the underlying stock, (6) the expiration month, (7) the strike (exercise) price, (8) the order price, and (9) the time limit (day or GTC), and any special instructions.

Options Clearing Corporation (OCC): A central corporation (owned jointly by all exchanges that trade listed stock option contracts) that guarantees clearance of option transactions. The OCC's functions include (1) issuance of the option contracts, (2) guaranteeing performance of option contracts, (3) acting as a clearing facility for option transactions, (4) establishing rules and regulations regarding option transactions, and (5) preparing and distributing the OCC options prospectus.

options in a fast market: A situation that can occur when trading volume on an options exchange is very heavy or when volume is very heavy for a particular option. Normal reporting is not possible and the options are declared by an official of the exchange to be in a "fast market." Quotes lag behind trading and the specialist is not held responsible for reporting.

or better (OB): Trading instructions that are always understood with a limit order; the client wishes the order to be executed at the limit price or at a better price.

order: Legally enforceable written or verbal instructions from a client to his broker to buy or sell a stated quantity of a specific security at market price or at a specific price. The order may also include special trading instructions. *See*
all or none order
alternative order
at market
at the close order
at the open order
buy
buy limit
day order
discretionary order
do not reduce
don't know
either/or
fill or kill
firm
good until canceled
hit the bid
immediate or cancel
limit order
limit or market on close
limit or market on open
market
market on close
market on open
not held
open order
or better
participate
scale

sell
stop
stop limit
stop loss
switch
today only

original issue discount bond (OID): A bond that is offered below face value at the time of the initial offering. The difference between redemption price and original issue price must be treated as income (rather than capital gains) over the life of the bond.

OTC: *See* over-the-counter market.

out-of-the-money: (1) A call option contract for which the striking (exercise) price of the call is above the market price of the underlying security. (2) A put option contract for which the striking (exercise) price of the put is below the market price of the underlying security.

outside financing: Corporate issuance of debt or equity securities to raise funds for expansion rather than relying on corporate retained earnings.

outstanding option: An option contract that has been issued by the OCC and has not expired, been closed, or exercised.

outstanding stock: All ownership shares in a corporation that have been issued to the public, officers, and others and have not been reacquired or canceled by the corporation.

overallotting: In a public offering on a security, more shares are confirmed than are available in anticipation that some orders will not be confirmed by the investors.

overbought: The price of a stock exceeds the established resistance levels due to heavy buying. The price is extended and there is a good probability that a subsequent decline in price will occur.

overcapitalized: Situation where the capital stock of a corporation is valued at a dollar amount greater than the value of the corporate assets.

oversold: The price of a stock exceeds the established trend on the downside due to heavy selling. The price is extended and there is a good probability that a subsequent upward movement will occur.

oversubscribed: Situation where investors have placed orders for shares in a public offering in excess of the number of shares available. It is usually allocated on a first-come basis or by cutting the number of shares included in each buy order.

over-the-counter market (OTC): A process for handling trades for securities not listed on a registered stock exchange. The trades are handled through negotiation among dealers who make a market in a particular security rather than by an auction system of a stock exchange. Most new issues and smaller issues are handled through the OTC market.

over-the-counter options: *See* unlisted options.

owner's equity: *See* net worth.

Pacific Stock Exchange: This exchange has two locations. Addresses: 618 South Spring Street, Los Angeles, California 90014, and 301 Pine Street, San Francisco, California 94104.

paid in surplus: A balance sheet entry in the Shareholder's Equity section that shows the difference between dollar value received on the actual issuance of shares and the par or stated value of those shares.

painting the tape: An illegal practice whereby matched orders are entered, with no real change in benefical owner, to create the illusion of heavy trading in a particular security. This is considered manipulation of the market and is illegal.

P & L statement: Profit and loss accounting statement issued by a corporation, showing sources of income and expense and net profit or loss. *See* income statement.

panic: Lack of confidence in the economy by the general public which can trigger or increase a period of recession or depression, and also resulting in heavy selling of securities.

paper: Generally refers to short-term notes such as commercial paper issued by corporations and banks.

paper loss: A decrease in the market value of a security below the price at which it was purchased. It is an unrealized (paper) loss until the security is liquidated.

paper profit: An increase in the market value of a security above the price at which it was purchased. It is an unrealized (paper) gain until the security is liquidated.

par: *See* par value.

parent corporation: One company that owns all or a majority of another company. The investing company is called the parent corporation and the other is called the subsidiary. Both corporations may operate as separate legal entities.

parity: Equality. When one item that may be converted for another is equal to their rate of conversion. For example, when a convertible bond and stock are both trading at a market price equal to their conversion ratio; or when the premium of an option plus its exercise price equals the current market value of the underlying security.

partial covered writing: An option position in which there is a combination of both covered and uncovered calls written against the same underlying security.

partial execution: Execution of a portion of a multiple round lot order. A partial execution must be accepted by the client unless he gives specific instructions to the contrary at the time the order is placed. *See* all-or-none order.

participate but do not initiate: Trading instructions often given when a large order is involved, requesting that the order should not initiate market activity but that it may be filled out of the normal market trading. This is often used by institutions to avoid having an adverse price effect on the market price of the security.

participating bond: A type of industrial bond that combines debt and equity participation to the holder. The holder will be paid the normal interest due and may share in dividends out of corporate earnings if profit permits.

participating brokers/dealers: Brokers and dealers who are not part of an underwriting syndicate but participate in the selling of a new offering. They are also called the selling group or selling concession.

participating exchange: A national securities exchange approved by the Securities and Exchange Commission to trade listed options that are issued by the Options Clearing Corporation.

participating preferred stock: A rare feature on some preferred stocks that allows the shareholders to participate in additional dividends after the regular preferred dividends and common stock dividends have been paid.

partnership: An unincorporated business owned by two or more persons known as partners. The agreement between the owners is usually set forth in a partnership agreement that specifies such matters as percentage of ownership, division of profits, dissolution, and responsibilities of the partners.

par value: Face value or nominal value. The dollar value assigned per share when issued, as stated in the corporate charter and printed on the face of certificate. Par value is the minimum price at which a share may be issued and be fully paid. Today most shares have a par value of $1 or $5. The proceeds received from the sale of shares higher than par value result in paid-in surplus.

passed dividend: Omission of a regular dividend by keeping the earnings, if any, in the corporation. This may indicate financial difficulty or it may just mean the corporation has decided to use internal funds for expansion rather than issuing additional stocks or bonds.

patent: An official license issued by the government giving the holder a non-renewable monopoly on the use of a new invention, device, process, or design. It is an intangible asset having a limited economic life.

payback period: The length of time required for a capital investment to return the amount invested.

payment date: The official date on which money, stock or other distributions to shareholders will be disbursed. Date of payments follows the date of record as specified in the dividend announcement. *Also called* distribution date.

payout: The annual proportionate amount of corporate earnings that are disbursed to shareholders as dividends.

payout ratio: The amount of dividends per share stated as a percentage of annual earnings per share. For example, if a corporation earns $3.00 per share and pays a dividend of $.50 per share, it has a payout ratio of 16.6 percent.

PC: *See* professional corporation.

P/E: *See* price/earnings ratio.

peak: A term used in retrospect to indicate the highest price that a stock or market indicator reached for a given period of time. It must, therefore, be followed by a period of decline.

pegging the market: An action used in some underwritings whereby the underwriters set up a fund to stabilize the price of the stock by means of a fixed bid at the offering price during the initial stages of the offering. Pegging the price, except in conjunction with a distribution, is manipulation and considered illegal.

penny stock: Term used for stocks that sell at extremely low prices. Most major brokerage firms consider any stock selling for less than $3.00 per share a penny stock. In most cases, these are speculative in nature and trade in the over-the-counter market.

pension plan: A plan established by an employer or the government for the payment of funds to disabled and retired employees. There are many varieties in format and structure of pension plans, but in most cases the employee is taxed only as funds are received.

P/E ratio: Terms frequently used for price/earnings ratio. It is the ratio between market price and earnings per share. *Also called* P/E multiple. *See* price/earnings ratio.

performance fund: A mutual fund that concentrates its investments in more speculative common shares. Higher risk is accepted in hopes of achieving very short-term growth in capital.

performance stock: Issues that are expected to show strong short-term growth in market price.

periodic payment plan: A plan offered by many mutual funds for the purchase of additional shares of the fund at regular intervals. *Also called* accumulation plan.

perpendicular spread: *See* vertical spread.

perpetual bond: A bond that has no maturity date or is so long-lived it is considered perpetual. It will continue to pay interest indefinitely.

per share net: After tax earnings of a corporation divided by the total number of common shares outstanding.

petrodollars: Large dollar balances, arising from sales by oil-producing countries, deposited in financial institutions throughout the world. *Also called* petrocurrency.

Philadelphia plan: One method for transferring ownership of equipment bought with equipment trust certificates. The title to the equipment is held by the trustee until the debt is retired in full. *See* equipment trust certificates. Compare New York plan.

Philadelphia Stock Exchange (PBW): Address: 1900 Market Street, Philadelphia, Pennsylvania 19103.

pink sheets: A list of over-the-counter stocks (including those not quoted on the NASDAQ System) showing the name of the corporation, trading symbol if available, the latest bid and ask prices and the names of the brokers or dealers making a market in each stock. This list is published daily by the National Quotation Bureau.

placement: The issuance of debt or equity securities through a public offering or private distribution.

plateau: A period of sideways price movement following a period of advancing prices. It indicates a period of uncertainty, but is often followed by a period of declining prices.

plow back: Retention of corporate earnings for use in the business rather than distribution in the form of dividends.

plunge: A quick sharp drop in the price of a security in a single day or two, which may indicate an immediate buy signal if other technical and fundamental factors are favorable.

plunger: One who invests heavily (plunges) into speculative situations.

plus tick: A transaction that occurs at a higher price than the previous transaction. *Also called* uptick.

PNI: *See* participate but do not initiate.

point: A unit of measure in reporting security prices. Generally, one point equals one percent. In quoting bonds, one point is one percent of the face value (usually $10). In mortgages, one point equals one percent. In the case of stocks, however, one point equals $1, and in reporting market indicator figures one point merely equals a one-point move from the base level.

point and figure chart: A method of depicting market price changes and the direction of those changes. Volume is not a consideration and time is not precisely measured.

portfolio: The total sum of all holdings, including cash, owned by investors or investment companies. A portfolio may be designed for growth, speculation, income, tax considerations, or a combination of the above.

position: The nature of holdings in an investment acount. Ownership of stocks or bonds or contracts is considered a long position. A short position is one in which shares or contracts have been sold short. Often accounts have both long and short positions which will minimize some of the risk and possibly minimize potential return.

position limits: Rule of the options exchanges that state no investor, or group of investors acting together, may hold more than 2,000 call or put contracts on the same underlying stock on the same side of the market. For example, the investor could hold 2,000 long calls and 2,000 long puts; but he could not hold 2,000 long calls and 2,000 short puts.

post: *See* trading post.

Post 30: A special trading post on the floor of the New York Stock Exchange where inactive stocks and shares traded in round lots of less than 100 shares are traded.

pot: Shares of a new issue that are reserved for filling institutional orders.

power of attorney: A legal and notarized document giving full legal authority to one party to act for the signatory party. Power of attorney is usually limited in scope.

preemptive right: The right given to existing shareholders to maintain their proportionate share of ownership in a corporation. When planning a new issue, the corporation will often first offer the shares to existing shareholders before offering shares to the general public. The right is evidenced by subscription rights that the shareholder may exercise, sell, or allow to expire.

preference stock: Preferred stock that has preference over subsequent issues of preferred stock and all common stock in the payment of dividends and distribution of proceeds in the event of liquidation. *Also called* prior preferred stock. *See* preferred stock.

preferred dividend coverage: The ratio of corporate after-tax income to annual dividends payable to preferred shareholders.

preferred stock: An equity security that ranks above common shares in the payment of dividends and claims on the assets of a corporation. Preferred shares combine features of common stock and corporate bonds in that they combine equity ownership with a fixed rate of return. Preferred stocks usually have a stated or par value and no voting rights and tend to move in market value according to changing interest rates.

preferred stock funds: Mutual funds that concentrate their investments in preferred stocks with the primary objective of higher current income and preservation of capital.

preliminary official statement: Similar to a preliminary prospectus. Preliminary statement issued for municipal securities offering that gives details about the upcoming offering.

preliminary prospectus: Often called red herring. A registration statement used for information purposes only that gives some details on a forthcoming new issue—but is not an offer to sell. It must have SEC approval before distribution. The preliminary prospectus does not contain the proposed offering price, it is not complete or final in all details, and it must be replaced by the final prospectus.

premium: (1) An amount above list price or face value. (2) The amount a bond is selling for above its face value. (3) The amount a preferred stock is selling for above its par value. (4) The amount by which a new security issue exceeds its offering price shortly after issuance. (5) The money that the writer (seller) of a stock option receives from the holder (buyer); it is the price at which option contracts are bought and sold. *Compare* discount.

premium bond: Any bond that is selling at a current market price that is above face value. The sum above face value is called the premium. *Compare* discount bond.

present value: (1) The worth of an item (investment) today, based on one or a series of future benefits. (2) The amount that must be invested today at a fixed compounded rate of interest to grow to $1.00 at the end of a set period of time.

price alert: A price breakout that takes place when a stock exceeds its highest or lowest price during a specific time period. The total number of stocks that have upside or downside breakouts can be used as a measure of strength or weakness in the market.

price averaging: Purchasing equal share amounts of a security at varying price levels. For example, an investor would purchase 200 shares of XYZ at $20, at $18, and at $24, for an average price of $20.67 per share.

price/dividend ratio (P/D): Calculated by dividing current market value per share by the annual dividend per share. This shows the relationship between the current market price of a stock and its annual dividend.

price/earnings ratio: The relationship between the current market price of a stock and its annual earnings per share. The P/E ratio is calculated by dividing current market price by annual earnings per share. P/E ratios are also calculated by industry group, for an exchange and for market averages. A stock selling at $30 per share and earning $3 per share has a P/E ratio of 10. This indicates investors are willing to pay 10 times the annual earnings to own shares in that corporation. The P/E ratio reflects how investors view the potential growth of earnings.

price index: A measurement of the degree to which prices for various goods and services have risen or fallen in comparison to a base period or previous period.

price potential: An estimate using technical analysis of a securities future market value. This may be a near, intermediate, or long-term price appraisal.

price range: The high and low limits within which a security has traded for a given time period. The price range may be quoted for a day or a year or the last 52 weeks.

price spread: (1) The difference between the asked price and bid price for any given security. (2) A stock option spread position involving the simultaneous purchase and sale of option contracts on the same underlying stock with the same expiration dates, but having different striking (exercise) prices. *Also called* vertical spread or money spread.

price/volume alert: A price breakout in which a stock exceeds its highest or lowest price during a specific period that is accompanied by a volume breakout. This indicates extremely forceful stock activity.

primary distribution: The initial distribution of any stock or bond issue that is used to raise capital for the issuing corporation. The typical procedure is to work through an investment banker who forms an underwriting syndicate to market the issue of securities.

primary market: The market that is composed of all investors who buy a new security offering in which the proceeds of the sale go to the issuing corporation.

primary offering: The initial sale of a company's securities to the public.

prime rate: The interest rate that major banks charge their most creditworthy corporate borrowers on short-term loans. Prime rate is used as a guide for setting other interest rates and offers an indication of economic conditions. Prime rate reflects both current conditions and expectations of future trends.

principal: (1) The amount of money committed to an investment on which earnings such as interest or dividends will be paid. (2) The face amount of a bond, note, or loan. (3) A dealer who buys or sells securities for his own account. (4) A major shareholder of an enterprise.

prior lien bond: A debt obligation that ranks ahead of other issues of the same issuing corporation.

prior preferred stock: A class of preferred stock that takes precedence over any subsequent preferred stock and all common stock issued by a corporation in the distribution of dividends and claims on assets.

private distribution: The distribution of a corporation's securities to a limited number of investors.

privately owned corporation: A corporation that is owned by one or a few shareholders most of whom are directly involved in the operation of the business. *Also called* closed corporation.

private offering: Offering for sale a new issue of securities to a limited number of investors. A private offering is usually limited to $300,000 or less and may not be offered to more than 25 investors.

private placement: A security offering or large block of shares that is placed through private negotiation. The issue may be sold to just one or two large institutional clients such as a bank or insurance company.

Producers Price Index: An index that measures change in the price of goods that are sold to the final user—either individuals or businesses. This index is used to measure the trend of inflation.

professional corporation: A corporation formed to practice a professional trade, such as law or medicine.

profit: (1) The gain from an investment that may be realized or unrealized. (2) The income from a business operation. It may be quoted before taxes, after taxes, for a single division, and so on.

profit and loss statement: Financial report issued quarterly and annually by a corporation that lists all sources of income and expenses and the net profit or loss. *See* income statement.

profit sharing plan: A fund set up for the benefit of employees to share in the profits of the corporation. There are numerous variations to this type of plan.

profit taking: Selling a security to take a profit in a strong market once the price has risen above purchase price (plus covering the cost of commission.) Widespread profit taking often occurs in stock after a sharp rise in market price; this may cause a dip for a few days, after which the price will usually resume its upward movement.

projection: To forecast future prices or conditions based on past data and assumed future conditions.

project notes (PN): Short-term debt obligations issued by the government to provide funds for public housing construction. The notes are guaranteed by the Department of Housing and Urban Development. When construction is completed, permanent bonds are issued to retire and replace the project notes.

proprietorship: A business entity owned by one person. The business is not incorporated and does not have shareholders. The owner is liable for all expense and debts and receives all profits.

prospectus: (1) A formal statement required by the Securities Act of 1933 that describes all facts and figures pertaining to a security issue being offered for public sale. The document must be issued to each prospective buyer of a public offering. The purpose of the prospectus is to insure complete disclosure of material regarding the company, its financial position, products, officers, litigations, the cost of the offering, and the proposed use of the funds from the offering. The prospectus that must be filed with the SEC is also called an offering circular. (2) See OCC prospectus.

proxy: A signed authorization given by a stockholder allowing another person to vote in his place for or against directors and other business proposed at the annual meeting or any other special votes. Most shareholders delegate their votes to management through a proxy.

proxy fight: A contest between two or more factions of shareholders including present directors. Each side tries to solicit signed proxies from other shareholders favoring its position to gain a voting majority. Often these proxy votes will decide which side will win control of management.

proxy statement: A statement issued by a corporation to its shareholders that explains the issues to be voted upon at the upcoming stockholders' meeting. The SEC requires this statement be sent in the solicitation of proxy votes.

prudent man rule: State-by-state acceptable standards that guide persons who control investments for others. The prudent man rule basically requires that the fiduciary use discretion and conservatism when investing for others and to avoid all types of speculation.

public corporation: The term generally means a corporation that has issued stock through a public offering and whose shares are traded on the open market. However, under certain regulations, two shareholders or more would constitute a public corporation. In other regulations 25 or fewer shareholders would constitute a private corporation. *Also called* publicly owned corporation.

Public Housing Authority Bond (PHA): Longer-term debt securities issued by municipalities to provide permanent financing for low- and middle-income housing.

public offering: An offering of a new issue of securities to the public. The process is usually handled by an underwriting syndicate and must meet all SEC and state registration requirements.

public utility: An economic unit that supplies a basic service to the general public such as telephone service, electric power, natural gas, water and—in some cases—transportation. These companies tend to operate as monopolies and therefore are highly regulated by the goverment.

public utility bond: Generally high-quality debt instruments issued by public utility companies. The bonds are usually backed by mortgages on buildings and equipment.

public utility stocks: Equity shares issued by public utilities which usually pay a high yield and are considered stable and safe due to their regulated status.

purchasing power: The amount of goods and services a given unit of currency can buy at current prices in comparison to a previous or base period.

put: *See* put option contract.

put option contract: A contractual agreement that gives the holder the right to sell, and the writer the obligation to buy, 100 shares of the underlying security per contract at a stated strike (exercise) price within a specific period of time.

put spread: An option spread position created by writing a put contract and purchasing a put contract on the same underlying security with different expiration dates, different exercise prices, or both.

put to: The right of a put option buyer to sell, in 100 share lots, a particular stock at a specific price to the writer who has sold an option contract on that stock. *See* exercise.

pyramiding: Increasing security holdings by using maximum buying power available in a margin account through paper profits and realized profits.

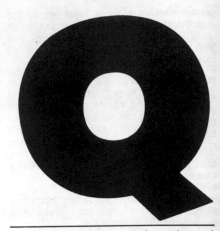

qualified employee stock options: A program offered by many corporations that allows employees to buy shares in their corporation at a fixed price within a specified period of time. If the purchase is not made within that period of time, the option will expire.

quality rating: A rating given to a security based on the financial structure and strength of the corporation, the history of paying dividends and interest, management ability, and other factors. The two most widely recognized rating services are Standard and Poor's, and Moody's.

quasi-public corporation: A privately owned corporation that has a high level of public responsibility and therefore is regulated by the government. An example would be a nonpublic utility company.

quick assets: Cash and cash equivalents plus receivables. This does not include inventory but does include government securities and other liquid securities. It is a quick method to calculate a company's ability to pay current liabilities.

quick ratio: A financial ratio calculated by dividing cash and cash equivalents plus accounts receivable by current liabilities. The term acid ratio is often used for this calculation which mea sures the short-term liquidity of a company.

quick turn: A security purchase that is followed by an almost immediate sale in order to make a short-term (quick) profit.

quotation: A firm price for any given security at that moment. It is the highest bid and lowest offer prices. The difference between the bid and offer is the spread.

quotation board: A display board where current daily market prices are posted either electronically or by the use of clip-on numbers. It usually shows the ticker symbol, number of shares traded, and the last trade price. But it may also include high, low, and open prices, and the previous trading day's closing price.

quote: Same as quotation. A quote of 25 1/4 to 25 1/2 means that $25.25 is the highest price any investor wishes to pay at the particular time for that stock and $25.50 is the lowest price anyone is willing to sell for at the same time. The difference between the bid and offer is the spread.

aid: (1) Illegal manipulation in which two or more persons cause the market

receiver's certificate: Certificates which represent the debt and equity securities of a corporation which has gone into receivership (a form of bankruptcy). The certificates are often traded on the open market.

receivership: One form of bankruptcy which allows reorganization. A trustee is appointed by the courts to oversee the reorganization and to resolve the financial problems of the corporation.

recession: A period of economic slump throughout the economy which is accompanied by high unemployment, high interest rates, declining stock prices and lower corporate profits. A calculation often used to determine a recession is a period in which gross national product declines for more than two quarters in succession.

record date: The date on which the investor must be registered on the books of the corporation as owner of record in order to receive a declared dividend, vote on company affairs, receive a stock split, or any other distribution or consideration.

recovery: A period of established advancing prices that follows a period of market decline or inactivity.

redeem: (1) Process by which note or bondholders are paid face value of their instruments at maturity. The issuing corporation buys back the bond/note which releases them of any further obligation. (2) The repurchase of mutual fund shares from the investors by the issuing fund.

redeemable bond: A bond that is issued with the provision that the issuing corporation may buy back the bond before maturity. In most cases, the bondholder will receive face value plus a premium to compensate for loss of future interest.

redemption price: The total price (face value plus any premium) at which an issuer will redeem a callable security.

price of a security to drop. (2) To buy controlling interest in an organization with the intent of using or channeling the assets and profits into another organization.

R & D: *See* research and development.

rally: A relatively short, strong rise in price following a period of decline or inactivity.

RAN: *See* revenue anticipation bond.

random walk theory: Theory which suggests that stock prices follow a random pattern because each price is independently or randomly determined in the auction market process.

ranking: Appraisal of a security's price performance during a specific period of time relative to all other securities being ranked.

rate of return: The annual after-tax profit stated as a percentage of capital investment. Calculated by dividing net income by stockholders equity, it is a measure of profitability.

rating of securities: An assessment of the financial strength and stability of a corporation. Ratings are based on management performance, growth and stability of earnings, debts, dividend payment record, and many other factors. Such ratings are not an attempt to recommend the purchase or sale of a security. The two most widely known rating services are Standard & Poor's, and Moody's.

ratio analysis: Analyzing and interpreting ratios that express certain figures as percentages of other figures or against minimum standards.

ratios: A tool used in the evaluation of statistical data. Data is compared by dividing one value into another producing a ratio. Ratios are then compared against past data, set standards, or other averages.

ratio spreading: A spread option strategy involving the simultaneous purchase and sale of option contracts on the same underlying security in which the number of contracts sold varies from the number of contracts purchased. *See* variable spread.

reacquired stock: Shares that were once issued by the corporation to shareholders and then subsequently repurchased by or given back to the corporation.

reaction: A movement in a price that is opposite a previous strong or lengthy movement. It is believed the previous sharp move up or down has departed from the norm and this movement is a stabilizing action.

real estate investment trust (REIT): A trust which offers its shares to investors and invests the funds received in real estate holdings.

realize: To actually take a profit or incur a loss upon the sale of a security. Until the sale takes place, the profit or loss is considered paper or unrealized gains or losses.

recapitalization: To change the financial structure of a corporation by adding more capital through the sale of additional debt or equity securities.

receding market: A period of generally declining prices. Usually indicated by most averages being down, this reflects a lack of enthusiasm among investors to add money to the markets. This can be a result of poor economic conditions, declining corporate profits, high interest rates, or other negative factors.

red herring: A preliminary statement that is distributed to potential investors of a new security offering. It reveals most of the details of an offering however, it is incomplete and must be replaced by the final prospectus. The red herring must receive SEC clearance before distribution and does not offer the security for sale. *Also called* preliminary prospectus.

rediscount rate: *See* Federal Reserve discount rate.

refinancing: *See* refunding.

reflex rally: An upward change in the direction of a price trend which does not reverse the established trend but instead corrects an oversold condition. *Compare* reflex reaction.

reflex reation: A downward change in the direction of a price trend which does not reverse that established trend but instead corrects an overbought condition. *Compare* reflex rally.

refunding: The sale of a new issue of bonds or stock where the proceeds are used to pay off existing debt securities. Refunding is used to reduce interest costs or to extend the maturity date or both.

regional fund: A mutual fund that concentrates its investments in the securities of companies located in a specific geographical area of the country or the world.

regional stock exchanges: Term used for national securities exchanges located outside of New York City. These exchanges typically list local issues which may or may not be listed on another exchange. *See* National Securities Exchange.

register: (1) To formally submit information to and receive clearance from the Securities and Exchange Commission and/or state agencies as required regarding the issuance of a new security and its subsequent sale to the public. (2) To formally record the names of shareholders on the books of a corporation.

registered bond: A bond registered in the name of the owner—both on the face of the bond certificate and on the corporate records. The bond is nonnegotiable until endorsed by the owner. *Compare* bearer bond.

registered competitive market maker: A member of the New York Stock Exchange who may act as a floor broker and execute trades for his own member firm or other member firms.

In addition, he or she must make a bid or offer on any stock traded on the floor, if so requested, to insure the maintenance of a fair and orderly market.

registered coupon bond: A bond registered in the name of the owner but for which the interest coupons are not registered and are negotiable merely by delivery. The coupons must be presented to a disbursing agent for payment of interest.

registered investment company: *See* regulated investment companies.

registered options principal (ROP): An employee of a member firm who is responsible for option transactions placed by customers of that firm.

registered over-the-counter stock: Unlisted, over-the-counter security that has been approved for trading in a margin account.

registered representative: An employee of a member firm who has passed all registration requirements and whose primary responsibility is to handle buy or sale orders for clients of the firm; in addition he or she may solicit accounts for investment advisory or investment management services. The registered representative is commonly called a stockbroker or customer's broker. *Also called* account executive.

registered stock: (1) Stock that has been formally filed with the Securities and Exchange Commission and/or state agencies for sale to the public. (2) Shares registered on the books of the corporation as to holder of record.

registered traders: Members of the exchange who use their floor trading privileges simply to buy and sell for their own account and those in which they have an interest. Their transactions must meet certain exchange requirements. *Also called* floor traders.

registrar: The formal recordkeeper. In most cases a bank or trust company will act as registrar and is responsible for checking the accuracy of any activity that has to do with the issuance of stock certificates. In some cases, the transfer agent and the registrar may be one and the same.

registration: *See* register.

registration statement: The statement filed with the Securities and Exchange Commission that contains all pertinent information regarding a corporation's sale of securities to the public.

regular-way settlement: Normal settlement of a security transaction; that is, delivery of certificates and payment of funds due no later than the fifth business day following that transaction date. Saturdays, Sundays, and certain holidays are not considered business days. Many other securities have a next business day settlement—such as option transactions.

regulated investment companies: Companies organized for the purpose of investing money for other people. The dollars are obtained by selling shares of the investment company to the public. The proceeds from the sale of shares may then be invested in any manner desired consistent with the company's charter and subject to regulations of the Investment Company Act of 1940. At least 90 percent of the profits of the investment company must be distributed to its shareholders. Most investment companies are called mutual funds and investment trusts. They may be open-end or closed-end companies and may be front-end load or no load.

Regulation A: Regulation governing the registration of a security offering of more than $50,000 but less than $300,000. It requires the use of a prospectus, but one that is less complicated than for public offerings of more than $300,000.

Regulation G: Regulation governing the amount of credit that may be advanced for the purchase of securities in circumstances that are otherwise unregulated.

Regulation Q: Regulation governing the maximum interest rate that Federal Reserve member banks may pay on regular savings accounts.

Regulation T: Regulation governing the amount of credit that may be advanced by brokers or dealers to their clients for the purchase of securities.

Regulation T-Call: *See* margin call.

Regulation U: Regulation governing the amount of credit that may be advanced by a bank to its customers for the purchase of securities.

rehypothecation: The pledging of securities by a brokerage firm in order to borrow funds to finance the purchase of securities in client margin accounts.

reinvestment: The investment of dividends and capital gains into additional shares of a mutual fund or other security. Most mutual funds and many common stock issues offer automatic reinvestment programs.

REIT: *See* real estate investment trust.

relative strength: A measure of the market performance of a security in comparison to its own industry and/or a market index for a specific period of time. Good relative strength is indicated if the stock's performance is better than that of the group to which it is being compared. For example, a relative strength ranking of 91 would show that the stock performed better than 91 percent of the group against which it is being compared.

reorganization: A form of involuntary bankruptcy that allows the corporation to continue operating. The financial structure is changed and management is replaced by a court appointed trustee in an attempt to solve the financial difficulties. This is Chapter 10 of the bankruptcy laws.

repurchase: Redeeming of shares from an investor by an issuer.

research & development (R&D): Corporate efforts to find and develop new products, processes, or production methods and the improvement of existing products and processes. There have been studies to indicate there is a direct relationship between dollars spent for R&D and rate of growth.

reserve requirement: The amount of money that member banks of the Federal Reserve System must hold in cash or on deposit with the Federal Reserve System. *See* Federal Reserve bank reserve requirement.

resistance level: A price level at which a sufficient supply of stock is potentially available to halt any further increase in price. Supply will exceed demand and temporarily halt or reverse an advance. *Compare* support level.

restricted account: A margin account in which the equity has fallen below the Regulation T initial margin requirement.

retained earnings: Earnings that are reinvested back into a business for expansion and working capital after having paid all expenses, taxes, interest, and dividends to shareholders. *Also called* surplus or earned surplus.

retail broker: *See* account executive, registered representative.

retire: (1) The issuer withdraws a security from the market, cancels it, and does not allow it to be resold or distributed. (2) To redeem a debt security at maturity or prior to maturity.

retired stock: Treasury shares or outstanding shares that have been called-in and canceled. The shares are removed from the list of authorized shares and can no longer be sold or distributed.

retirement accounts: *See* individual retirement account, Keogh plan.

return: The dividend or interest received on an investment. It is stated as a percentage of acquisition price or current market price.

return of capital: Cash payments to shareholders that are considered a return of invested capital rather than distribution of dividends. This is a nontaxable event but the investor must reduce the original cost of investment by the amount returned.

return on investment (ROI): Relationship between total profit and investment, calculated by dividing pretax income by the amount of the investment.

revenue anticipation note (RAN): A short-term note issued by an municipality to finance a project that will usually be repaid and replaced by a longer-term municipal revenue bond or specific revenues.

revenue bond: A municipal bond issued by authorities or commissions to build income producing facilities where the income generated by the project is used to pay the interest and principal. An example would be a toll bridge.

reversal: A change in the near-term direction of market price that continues for several days. If the change is from advancing to declining, it is called a down-reversal. It is called an up-reversal if the change is from declining to advancing.

reversal pattern: Change in the direction of a security's market price.

reverse split: Dividing the number of shares authorized to a lesser number. Shareholders continue to maintain their proportionate ratio of ownership but it is represented by fewer shares. For example, in a five for one reverse split, a shareholder previously owning 1,000 shares would then own 200 shares.

rigging: Manipulation of stock prices by such means as wash sales, publicizing false information, and so on. Such practices are considered illegal.

rights: Option given to existing shareholders of a corporation to purchase a specified number of shares within a

95

specific time period. Rights usually expire within a relatively short period of time. The shareholder may exercise his option, trade them on the open market, or let them expire.

rights offering: The use of subscriptions to sell a new security issue to existing shareholders before the issue is offered to the general public. Usually one right is issued for each share held.

rights of shareholders: Being the legal owners of a corporation, shareholders have certain rights, which are stated in the corporate charter. These include the right to vote on certain corporate matters, to vote for the board of directors, to amend the charter, to approve a mortgage on assets of the corporation, to approve a merger, to approve a reorganization of the company, to approve dissolving the corporation, to receive their share of declared dividends or assets upon the dissolution of the company, and to receive a certificate showing ownership and be allowed to transfer that ownership at will.

risk: The possibility of loss. It is the unknown factors of future values and future events. Risk is often calculated as percentage of probability.

risk capital: Another term for invested capital or equity capital. These are the funds invested in the equity ownership of a company.

risk of capital: The risk that all or a portion of one's original investment will be lost.

risk of inflation: The risk that the return of principal on an investment will have lower buying power than when the investment was originally made or that the yield on an investment will not keep pace with inflation.

risk of selection: The risk that the investor, given an equal choice of investment alternatives, will choose unwisely.

risk of timing: The risk that the investor will make investments at the wrong time according to market conditions.

risk/reward: The possible loss versus the possible gain on an investment. Risk/reward is usually expressed as a ratio. For example, if a stock is currently at $20 and it is believed it could rise to $30 or fall to $15, the ratio is 2:1.

ROI: *See* return on investment.

rolling over: The substitution of a far option for a near option on the same underlying security at the same striking price. For example, the option trader would close out a position that expires in January and buy the same option expiring in April.

rollover: (1) Applying the proceeds received from a maturing bond into a new bond issue of identical or nearly identical type. (2) Refunding of a debt obligation by issuing a new bond of identical or nearly identical type.

ROP: *See* registered options principal.

round lot: A standard unit of trading. A round lot is usually 100 shares in the case of stocks and $1,000 face value in bond. A few inactive shares have a standard unit of 10 or 25 or 50 shares.

round lot cash buy/sell ratio: Cash account buying of round lots divided by cash account selling of round lots. The ratio is generally around 1.50 at lows and drops below .80 at tops.

round lot margin buy/sell ratio: Margin account buying divided by margin account selling. The ratio is generally below .80 at intermediate term bottoms and around 1.50 at tops. Some analysts believe this ratio is now distorted since the introduction of money market margin accounts.

round lot short/cover ratio: Total round lot shares shorted divided by total shares covered. A reading of 2.00 indicates that twice as many shares were shorted as covered.

round trip: The completion of a cycle in buying and selling a security. The term also applies to short sales of stock and the covering of those same shares.

royalty: Income received for the use of one's property, product, or idea.

Rule of '78: A method for calculating interest refunds in the event of early payoff of a debt.

Rule 144: SEC rule covering the sale of control securities and restricted securities.

runaway inflation: A high rate of inflation that cannot be brought under control by normal means.

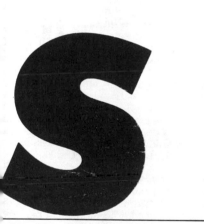

safety: The assumption that a loss will not occur. All investments contain a degree of risk. However, some investments have a higher relative degree of safety than other investment alternatives.

safety of income: The assumption that a corporation will continue to make interest and/or dividend payments on time.

safety of principal: The assumption that the dollars invested in shares of a company will remain relatively stable if not increase; or that a bond will be paid in full at maturity.

saucer pattern: A charted price pattern that shows little activity following a period of decline and then somewhat of

an upturn. Also called basing or base-building, it may be interpreted as the period needed for a stock to gather momentum for a rally.

same-day substitution: The practice of selling one security and buying another on the same trade date; normally the purchase and sale are of equal value.

sandwich spread: *See* butterfly spread.

savings and loan associations: National or state chartered financial institutions that accept savings deposits from their customers and loan the majority of receipts for real estate mortgages.

savings bond: A bond issued by the U.S. Treasury that is not traded on the open market and is redeemable only by the government. *See* Series EE Bonds and Series HH Bonds.

scaling: Practice where a series of buy or sell orders is placed by the investor at various specified prices or at market at different times rather than placing one single order for all the shares desired.

scrip: A certificate issued by a corporation that may be redeemed (usually within a specified time period) for stock, dividends or funds. This is often used when a split occurs and an individual is entitled to some fractional share.

scripophily: An interest in collecting old stock and bond certificates.

SDR: *See* special drawing rights.

seasonal trends: Pronounced advances and declines in the market for a relatively short period of time that have recurred fairly consistently, such as a "year-end rally."

seat: Membership on an exchange. Only members are permitted to trade on the "floor" of the exchange. A seat (membership) has sold for as high as $625,000 in 1929 and as low as $17,000 in 1942 on the NYSE. There are 1366 seats on the NYSE and 650 on the AMEX.

SEC: *See* Securities and Exchange Commission.

secondary distribution: The distribution of a large block of stock that has already been issued. The offering must be reregistered with and cleared by the SEC. The offering price is usually at or near current market price. A secondary distribution is used when an individual or institution or other corporation wants to sell a large block of stock without placing it directly on the market and possibly causing instability in price.

secondary market: (1) The after market. The supply and demand for a security once the initial offering is completed. *Compare* primary market. (2) Continuous exchange market for the purchase and sale of options that allows both holders and writers of outstanding positions to liquidate their open contracts by offsetting closing transactions.

second mortgage bond: A bond secured by a mortgage but subordinate to bonds secured by a first mortgage.

secular trends: The long-run trend of the market over a 10-, 25-, or 50-year period.

securities: Pledges of corporations used to raise funds for the purpose of meeting financial obligations. There are two broad classes of securities: debt and equity. Debt securities represent claims of creditors, and equity securities represent claims of owners.

Securities Act of 1933: Act of Congress that provides for registration of a security for public offering and for full and fair disclosure of material information on all initial security distributions. The SEC enforces the provisions of this act.

Securities Act of 1934: Act of Congress that regulates activities dealing with trading of outstanding shares. The act regulates securities exchanges and the over-the-counter market and those persons and firms involved in selling securities. The SEC enforces the provisions of this act.

Securities and Exchange Commission (SEC): Government agency set up by the Securities and Exchange Act of 1933 to regulate securities transactions. The SEC is empowered to set up rules and regulations, govern various aspects of the securities business and take necessary disciplinary action in the event of violations. Address: 500 North Capital Street, Washington, D.C. 20549.

Securities Investors Protection Corporation (SIPC): Government-sponsored membership insurance corporation designed to protect clients of SIPC member firms from certain losses should a member firm fail. All brokers and dealers registered with the Securities and Exchange Commission and all members of national stock exchanges are required to be members of SIPC. SIPC does not protect an investor from any loss due to fluctuations in market value. Address: 900 17th Street, N.W. Suite 800, Washington, D.C. 20006.

seller's market: Period when demand is high for a particular security or when investors' attitudes toward the markets are very good. The increasing demand pressure causes the market price to rise. *Compare* buyer's market.

seller's option trade: A form of settlement that gives the seller, at his option up to 60 days to deliver certificates in the completion of a transaction.

selling against the box: *See* short sale against the box.

selling concession: The brokers and dealers who aid in the distribution of an offering of securities. They have no liability in the underwriting and are paid on a commission basis. *Also called* the selling group.

selling group: *See* selling concession.

sell-off: A period of declining prices due to heavy selling pressure. It is more pronounced than profit taking and results from fear of future market decline.

selling on balance: Selling-off of securities on declining market price that is accompanied by high volume. Supply is greater than demand and surplus shares may be purchased by the specialists and dealers.

sell order: A written or verbal order given by a shareholder to a broker to liquidate a specific number of shares of a particular security at a specific price or at market with or without any other trading instructions.

sell-out: Process that occurs when the buyer of securities fails to accept delivery or settle the transactions by delivery funds by settlement date. The client buying the security would be liable for any unsettled balance.

sell signal: Technical indicators point to the fact that a stock is in a pattern that could soon lead to a down-reversal. *Compare* buy signal.

senior bond: A bond that ranks above other debt instruments in claims against the assets of the issuing corporation.

senior securities: The ranking of debt and equity securities in claims against the assets of an issuing corporation. Those having primary claim are most senior.

sentiment indicators: Market indicators that attempt to determine changes in investor psychology that affect investment decisions.

serial bond: A single bond issue offered at one time that has a portion maturing on successive dates until it is fully retired. *Compare* series bond.

series bond: A single bond issue that is offered on different dates to the public rather than one issuance date. *Compare* serial bond.

Series EE Bonds: Nontransferable U.S. Government savings bonds that are issued at a discount. Sold in denominations of $25 or more and maturing in seven to ten years.

Series HH Bonds: Nontransferable U.S. Government current income bonds that are sold at face value and pay interest semiannually. Sold in denominations of $500 or more and maturing in ten years.

series of options: All option contracts of the same class (either all calls or all puts) on the same underlying security having the same striking (exercise) price and the same expiration date.

sensitive market: A market in which investors react to financial or economic news.

session: A trading day on an organized exchange.

settlement: (1) To close out a brokerage account. (2) To complete a security transaction by delivering the required security certificates and/or funds.

settlement date: The day on which the required securities and/or funds must be deposited into the brokerage account for any security transaction. Sometimes called due date.

share: Proportional ownership in the equity of a corporation. Ownership is represented by a stock certificate.

shareholder: An individual or organization who owns shares in the ownership of a corporation. Ownership is represented by a stock certificate which may be delivered to the shareholder or held in a brokerage account. *Also called* stockholder.

shareholder's equity: *See* stockholder's equity.

shelf registration: Proper registration with the SEC to offer a security for sale at some date in the future that has not yet been determined.

short: To sell short is to sell securities that the investor does not own at a certain price in anticipation of buying back those same securities at a lower price. The profit or loss is the difference between purchase and sale prices. The seller's brokerage house will loan him the securities that must be delivered to the buyer. A short sale may only be made in a margin account.

short call: A call option contract that has been sold on an opening sale transaction. *Compare* short call.

short covering: To purchase securities to replace those that have been borrowed on a short sale.

short interest: (1) The number of shares sold short on the NYSE. A large volume of short sales indicates that many investors anticipate lower prices. It also represents potential buying power as short sellers buy back stock to cover their short positions. (2) Shares of stock that have been sold short but not yet repurchased to close out the short position.

short interest ratio: Ratio calculated by dividing the reported short interest (number of shares shorted on the NYSE) by the average NYSE volume for a 30-day period. A ratio above 1.60 is considered bullish and a ratio below 1.00 is considered bearish.

short market value (SMV): SMV is the current market value, calculated on a daily basis, of securities that have been sold short in a margin account.

short position: The position of an investor who has sold securities short, but has not yet covered those shares.

short put: A put option contract that has been sold on an opening sale transaction. *Compare* long put.

short sale: To sell short is to sell securities that the investor does not own at a certain price in anticipation of buying back those same securities at a lower price. The profit or loss is the difference between purchase and sale prices.

The seller's brokerage house will loan him the securities that must be delivered to the buyer. A short sale may only be made in a margin account.

short sale against the box: A short sale involving stock that is presently owned by the investor. The stock is sold as a short sale to lock in profits in the current year but to transfer capital gains tax liability to the following year. However, rather than buying back the shares as in a normal short sale, the investor will deliver the shares he already owns to cover his short position. *See* short/short sale.

short sale rule: SEC rule requiring all short sales to be made on an uptick or zero-plus tick.

short seller: Investor who has sold securities short in anticipation of covering those same securities at a lower price.

short squeeze: Being in a position of having to cover a short position at a higher price than the price for which it was sold and incurring a loss.

short term: Generally used in the securities markets to indicate a period of less than one year.

short-term capital gain: For taxes and accounting purposes, it is the profit received on an investment held for one year or less. The gain is treated as an addition to ordinary income.

short-term capital loss: For taxes and accounting purposes, this is a loss incurred on an investment held for one year or less. The loss is a deduction against ordinary income.

short-term trading: Buying securities and holding them only long enough to take advantage of short-term price fluctuations.

short-term trading index (TRIN): Advance/decline ratio divided by advancing/declining volume ratio. This figure is calculated for both the American Stock Exchange and the New York

tock Exchange once every minute and
s used for determining intraday move-
nents. Generally an index of 1.00 or
ess is considered bullish and an index
f 1.00 or more is considered bearish.

ignal: Technical indicators that show a
tock is in a pattern that should soon
ead to an important change in its
rend. These patterns may indicate
ither a buy signal or a sell signal.

ideways or neutral market: A period
n which prices show little change up or
own. The trading prices remain within
narrow range.

inking fund: Cash or cash equivalents
egularly set aside in a separate fund
usually held by an independent trus-
ee) that are to be used to redeem debt
ecurities or to retire preferred stock.

inking fund bond: Bond that is issued
vith the restriction on the issuer that a
inking fund be set up to insure repay-
nent of principal at maturity.

IPC: *See* Securities Investors Protec-
ion Corporation.

leeper: Usually used in retrospect to
escribe a stock that was underpriced
vith little investor interest that unex-
ectedly and sharply moves up in
rice.

low market: Sluggish market. Market
n which there is little trading activity
nd relatively minor changes in mar-
et price.

lump: (1) A temporary downturn in
narket prices. Declines are not severe
nd investor psychology is not in a
tate of panic. (2) Economy shows a
low-down in activity and an increase
n unemployment.

MA: *See* special miscellaneous
ccount.

mall investor: The average individual
nvestor. The term is used to describe
ndividual investors who buy a few to a
ew hundred shares per transaction.
'his is the largest group of investors

compared with institutions, corporations, and large individual investors;
however, they hold significantly fewer
shares than any other group.

smart money: A term used to describe
sophisticated investors that have greater investment knowledge and experience than the average investor. Therefore, these investors will continuously
move their investment dollars to the
most profitable situations.

SMV: *See* short market value.

sole proprietorship: An unincorporated
business organization owned by one
individual. This individual is responsible for all expenses and debts of the
company and receives all profits.

SOP: *See* statement of policy (mutual
funds).

sophisticated investor: The wealthy
individual investor who has a great
deal of market knowledge and experience and the time to study market
movements and opportunities. He is
able to invest large sums of money and
yet move it more quickly than institutions or corporations.

special assessment bond: Municipal
bond issued to fund a project, such as
the construction of sewers, that is
backed by taxes imposed upon those
within the project area.

special bond account: A separate
account set up by brokerage firms for
bookkeeping purposes to show the
amount of buying power available on
bonds bought on margin.

special drawing rights (SDRs): Commonly called paper gold, SDRs represent a credit in the International Monetary Fund that participating countries
may draw against to pay their balance
of payment deficits.

specialist: Member of the exchange
who makes a market in one or more
securities and presides over a trading
post. His function is to maintain a fair
and orderly market in those securities.

He is expected to risk his own capital by buying those securities at a higher price or selling at a lower price than the public may be willing to pay or accept at that moment. Each exchange sets specific regulations regarding specialists' activity.

specialist block purchase.: Transaction where the specialist purchases a large block of stock for his own account. This must follow regulations set by the exchange and not interfere in maintaining a fair and orderly market.

specialist block sale: Transaction where the specialist sells a large block of stock from his own account. This sale must follow regulations set by the exchange and not interfere in maintaining a fair and orderly market.

specialist's book: The book in which the specialist records all limit and stop orders for each security that have been left with him. The book also shows any market orders to sell short. Orders are logged according to price in the order in which the specialist receives them.

special miscellaneous account: A special account, for bookkeeping purposes, for use with a margin account that shows the amount of excess funds that are available to the customer, but that have not been withdrawn or used.

special situation: An individual security holds above average profit potential because of a special development (example: a merger announcement) regardless of the industry or present market conditions.

speculation: Investing in risky situations in hopes of significant capital appreciation in a short period of time.

speculation indicators: Market indicators that attempt to measure the amount of risk that investors are willing to take. Market peaks are usually accompanied by high speculation and market lows by lack of speculation.

speculative securities: Based on fundamental information, this rating describes securities issued by relatively new companies of unproven financial strength, market placement, management ability, and/or consistent performance, and by companies with less than average financial strength.

speculator: An investor who accepts higher risks in hopes of higher than average profits. This investor is generally knowledgeable in market activities and is able to weigh risks involved rather than just gamble. The speculator's investment process includes the use of leverage, margin buying, short selling, and so on.

spike: A sharp rise in price in a single day or two. The rise may be as great as 15 to 30 percent and may indicate an immediate sell signal.

spin-off: The creation of a new corporation by separating a division or subsidiary and transferring a portion of corporate assets and a portion of shareholder's equity to the new organization. Stockholders of the parent corporation will receive shares in the new corporation to maintain their proportion of original ownership.

split: Corporate action of dividing shares authorized into a larger number with a lower market value. Shareholders continue to maintain their proportion of ownership but it is represented by a greater number of shares. For example, in a two for one split a shareholder with 500 shares valued at $30 would then have 1,000 shares with market price of $15.

Spokane Stock Exchange: Address: 22 Peyton Building, Spokane, Washington 99201.

sponsor: The individual or individuals who perform the duties of the Board of Directors for an unincorporated mutual fund.

spot price: Commodity term used to indicate the price for a commodity that is due for immediate delivery.

102

spread: (1) The difference between the bid price and the asked price for a security. (2) An option position that involves the simultaneous purchase and sale of options within the same class on the same underlying security. They may have the same or different striking price with the same or different expiration months. *See* credit spread, debit spread.

stabilization: (1) A period of sideways price movement that usually occurs before a price changes direction. After a decline it is called basing or accumulation and after an advance it is called top-formation or distribution. (2) Legal manipulation called "pegging the market" that underwriters use to maintain the market price of a security immediately after a public offering so it does not drop below the offering price.

stabilizing bid: The bid price offered by underwriters of a new security offering used to maintain the market price of a security immediately after a public offering.

stagflation: A period of economic stagnation that is accompanied by inflation.

stagnation: A period of economic slowdown in which there is relatively little growth in GNP, capital investments, and real income.

Standard & Poor's: Commonly called S & P. Highly regarded investment advisory service and stock and bond rating service. Address: 343 Hudson Street, New York, New York 10014.

Standard & Poor's indices: The S & P indices are based on issues traded on the New York Stock Exchange. The averages are quoted in points and hundredths of points and are calculated by multiplying the price of each issue by the number of shares outstanding—therefore, more weight is given to larger issues, such as IBM and General Motors.

standardized expiration dates: All options issued by the OCC have fixed expiration dates that run in three-month cycles. There are three expiration cycles. *See* expiration cycle.

stated value: Calculated per share value assigned to shares of stock for accounting purposes. There is no relationship between stated value and market value.

statement: (1) Monthly summary of purchases, sales, holdings, and the month-end position of a cash or margin brokerage account. (2) A summary prepared to show the financial condition, revenues or losses, and position of a business organization.

statement of policy (SOP): A set of standards set forth by the Securities and Exchange Commission by which all investment companies must adhere. The SOP requires a conservative approach in management and sales of mutual funds, and requires full disclosure and explanation of risks and fees.

statutory voting: A shareholder voting method in which each shareholder is granted one vote for each share of stock held for each director to be elected. The shareholder may not give more than that number of votes to any one nominee. *Compare* cumulative voting.

stock: General term used to describe equity shares or ownership in a public or private corporation. Ownership of the same class is divided into equal value shares and proportionate ownership is represented by the number of shares held. Ownership is represented by a stock certificate showing the number of shares owned. Various terms are used to identify, classify, or clarify the term stock.

stock ahead: Situation where buy or sell orders have priority due to the time placed or the size over other bids or offers. The NYSE rules that for bids made at the same price, the bid made first has priority, followed by bids of equal or greater size than the amount of shares offered. Therefore an order may not be executed even though the record shows other trades being executed at that particular price and time.

stockbroker: *See* broker, registered representative.

stock certificate: The actual paper showing ownership of shares in a corporation. The certificate bears the name of the issuing company, the name of the shareholder, the name of the registrar, the par value and the number of shares represented by the certificate.

stock charts: *See* charting.

stock clearing corporation: A clearing agency that handles delivery of securities and payment of funds between member firms of an exchange.

stock dilution: *See* dilution.

stock dividend: A dividend paid in the form of additional shares of stock instead of cash. It is usually expressed as a percentage of shares held. *See* dividend.

stock exchange: A specific organized marketplace where buyers and sellers of securities may be brought together. It is the physical location where brokers and dealers transact security business for their clients. All exchanges admit only their own members to conduct business. *See* National Securities Exchange, Regional Stock Exchange.

stockholder: An individual or organization who shares in the ownership of a corporation. Ownership is represented by a stock certificate or shares held in street name. *Also called* shareholder.

stockholder of record: The stockholder whose name is registered on the books of the transfer agent as of the record date. The stockholder of record is the one entitled to any distribution of dividends, rights, and so on, that will be issued and the privilege to vote based on the record date.

stockholder proposal: A proposal made by a stockholder, who may or may not be an officer or other key person, which is brought before other stockholders at the annual meeting.

stockholder's equity: The interest of stockholders in a corporation that amounts to assets over liabilities. It is the net worth of a company.

stock market: (1) The actual supply and demand for a stock of a publicly held corporation. (2) Term often used in reference to the securities exchanges.

stock option: (1) Right offered by a corporation to certain key individuals, usually employees, to purchase a given number of shares of corporate stock within a specified time period and usually below current market price. (2) A contractual agreement between the holder (buyer) and the writer to purchase or sell shares of an underlying security, in 100-share lots, at a specific price within a predetermined period of time.

stock power: A legal document that gives authority to another party, such as a bank or brokerage firm, to transfer stock ownership to another name. It is sometimes used in place of signing the stock certificate for good delivery.

stock pricing: Stock prices are typically quoted in whole digits and fractional amounts. For example, a stock selling at 23 3/8 per share would be $23.375 for each share. A quote of up 5/8 of a point, would indicate the stock is trading at $.625 higher than the previous day's close.

stock purchase plan: Corporate benefit that enables employees to purchase corporate stock on a regular basis. The plan may include a reduction in commission costs, reduced purchase price, or corporate participation in the purchase. *See* employee stock ownership plan.

stock ratings: A method for evaluating the financial strength and/or management performance of a company issuing equity securities.

stock split: *See* reverse split, split.

stock tables: Figures appearing in the financial sections of papers that report market data. They usually give the high and low price for the year, the high, low, and closing price for the trading day, and the change from the close of the previous day. Most also include trading volume, price-earnings ratio, dividend payment, and yield.

stock ticker: A device that is rarely used today that prints stock trading data on a continuous narrow tape within seconds after the transaction takes place.

stop-limit order: A stop order and limit order combined. As soon as the market price occurs at the stop price, the order becomes a limit order to either buy or sell. *See* limit order, stop order.

stop-loss order: A stop order or stop-limit order that is placed at a price below current market price. The order is placed to protect a profit or minimize a loss.

stop order: A conditional market order to buy or sell a security that is designed to protect a profit or limit a loss. When the market price reaches the stop price it will activate a market order. The sell-stop order is placed below the current market price and is used to sell that stock at market if the price should start to fall. The buy-stop order is placed above the current market price and is used to buy the stock if the price should start to rise.

stopped stock: An order that has been temporarily guaranteed in price to a member by a specialist. It is a service that allows the member a short time to seek a more advantageous price, while being certain that the price quoted by the specialist will not rise. If no better price is found the member can take the guaranteed price from the specialist. *Also called* stopping stock.

straddle: An option position that involves the simultaneous purchase or sale of an equal number of both puts and calls on the same underlying security with the same expiration date and exercise price.

strap: A stock option position involving two calls and one put with the same expiration date and the same striking price.

street name: The registration of stock in the name of the brokerage firm or some other nominee rather than the shareholder's name. This is done to permit rapid transaction of business and ease when transferring securities from one owner to another.

strike price/striking price: The price per share at which the holder of a stock option contract may purchase the underlying security on a call option or sell the underlying security on a put option. *Also called* exercise price.

strip: A stock option position involving two puts and one call on the same underlying security with the same expiration date and the same striking price.

Sub-Charter M: Internal Revenue Service code that allows special tax treatment of regulated investment companies, providing a minimum of 90 percent of the investment company's income is distributed to its shareholders.

subject price: Estimated price quoted by a broker or dealer. It is not a firm quote or firm market and is subject to confirmation. *Also called* subject market.

subordinated debenture: A debt security that according to its terms of issuance ranks junior in payment of both principal and interest to one or more other securities of the issuing corporation.

subscriber: Securities investor who agrees to buy a stated number of shares of a new security offering.

subscription: An agreement of intention to buy a stated number of shares of a new security issue in a public offering.

subscription capital: The funds received by the issuer from a public offering of securities.

subscription price: The fixed asking price per share at which an issue of securities is offered to the public. During the offering the price is set and will not fluctuate.

subscription rights: *See* rights.

subscription warrant: *See* warrant.

subsidiary: A corporation that is wholly owned or subject to the direct control of another corporation. The controlling corporation is called the parent corporation.

suitability: The term used when investment recommendations and choices are appropriate and meet the investment objectives of the client taking into consideration the financial capability, temperament and other holdings of the client.

supply: The number of shares offered for sale at a particular time. *Compare* demand.

supply and demand indicators: Market indicators that attempt to measure the flow of funds into or out of the markets or groups of stocks.

support level: A price level at which sufficient demand for a stock is potentially available to halt any further decline in price. Demand exceeds supply and will temporarily halt or reverse a decline. *Compare* resistance level.

surplus: *See* retained earnings.

suspension: Penalty action against a brokerage firm or one of its employees if it has been determined that a violation of regulations has occurred. Suspension may last only a few days or weeks or may be permanent.

suspension of trading: Action taken by an exchange in which trading of a particular security is halted for a period of time in order to stabilize the market.

swapping: Exchanging securities in a portfolio, usually similar in amount, to change yield, coupon, maturity, or investment objectives. *See* tax swapping.

sweetener: Something of value added to a proposal. For example, an offering on bonds may have warrants attached that will enable the investor to buy stocks and thereby make the bond offering more attractive to potential investors.

switching: (1) In mutual funds, switching is the practice of selling shares in one fund and purchasing shares in another fund operated under the same family of funds. Switching among funds allows the investor to take advantage of changes in the investment climate. (2) Selling securities in a portfolio and replacing them with other securities. This allows investors to take advantage of changes in the investment climate.

switch order: An order to purchase one stock and sell another at the same time with a specific price difference.

symbol: A set of identifying letters assigned to a security to speed reporting of market activity. In print the symbols for NYSE and AMEX listed stocks appear as larger uppercase letters using one, two, or three letters. OTC stocks will usually be assigned four or five small uppercase identifying letters. *Also called* ticker tape symbol.

syndicate: The group of investment bankers joined together to underwrite and distribute a new security offering or large block of stock. They generally share risk by actually purchasing and then reselling the stock on the public offering.

TAB: *See* Tax Anticipation Bill.

takedown: The number of shares of a new offering that each member of an underwriting syndicate agrees to handle.

takeover: Assuming control of one corporation by another. It may be a friendly merger or an unwanted acquisition.

takeover arbitrage: Purchasing and/or selling the securities of companies involved in takeover situations in hopes of realizing a profit.

takeover candidate: A corporation that is currently being looked at as a takeover possibility by another corporation; or even one that is in the position for being taken over.

take up: To pay off the total balance due on a margined security, thereby having full ownership of that security.

taking a bath: To incur large losses on an investment.

TAN: *See* Tax Anticipation Note.

tangible assets: Assets that have a physical substance, such as equipment or tools, as opposed to intangible assets such as goodwill.

tangible value: The difference between the stiking price of a stock option con-

tract and the market price of the underlying security. *See* intrinsic value.

tape: Service offered by major exchanges that reports price and size of security transactions. *Also called* ticker tape or ticker.

target company: A corporation that has been selected by another corporation as a possible takeover candidate.

taxable event: An economic event that is subject to taxation, for example, receiving dividend or interest payments.

tax-advantaged investment: An investment with the principal feature that it is tax-free or tax-favored or will lower personal income tax liability.

Tax Anticipation Bill (TAB): Short-term debt instruments issued by the U.S. Treasury to meet very near term financial needs. These bills have largely been replaced with cash-management bills. *See* cash management bills.

Tax Anticipation Note (TAN): Short-term notes issued by municipalities to meet short-term financial needs that are scheduled to mature, in anticipation of tax receipts.

tax anticipation obligation: Any of the several debt instruments issued by the U.S. Government for the purpose of raising money in anticipation of tax revenue.

tax avoidance: Deductions, credits, and other IRS-approved methods that a taxpayer may use to reduce his tax liability. Proper financial planning and investments will create the possibility of tax avoidance. *Compare* tax evasion.

tax evasion: Not paying taxes that are properly due by falsifying tax records. Tax evasion is a criminal offense and includes such activities as not reporting all earned or unearned income, claiming false tax credits, claiming false deductions, and so on. *Compare* tax avoidance.

tax-exempt bonds: Debt securities issued by government municipalities that permit full or partial tax-free interest or dividend income to the holder.

tax-free instruments: Debt securities issued by the federal government, state or municipal agency on which the interest received is fully or partially free of federal and state income taxes.

tax selling: The strategy of selling securities at the end of a tax year if losses realized would reduce income tax liability and it is believed that the security will not move up significantly in value in the near term.

tax shelter: An investment opportunity approved by the IRS with provisions for tax-free or tax-favored income. Usually the purpose is to attract investors to higher risk investments such as oil drilling, agriculture, or real estate development.

tax swapping: Investment strategy in which investors sell one security at the end of the tax year in order to create a loss for tax purposes and then reinvest the proceeds into another security that the investor believes will show a higher potential for gain.

T-bill: *See* Treasury bill.

technical adjustment: A short-term change in the general trend of the market either up or down: It may be the result of an overbought or oversold condition or profit taking. It is an action or reaction by investors that can be seen as having a short-term stabilizing effect.

technical analysis: Examination and interpretation of market prices and indexes related to the actual supply and demand for securities. Charts and various indicators are used in an attempt to forecast future price movements. Technical analysis is usually concerned with near- to intermediate-term movements. *Compare* fundamental analysis.

technical analyst: A securities analyst who examines and interprets charts of stock prices and other market indicators and then makes forecasts based on these patterns and signals. *Compare* fundamental analyst.

technical correction: A short-term change in the direction of a trend. It occurs when fundamentals are strong (or weak) yet the market reverses direction for a short period of time. This break in the trend can be explained as a self-adjusting market movement.

technical indicators: Tools used by technical analysts in order to make predictions of future price movements. Technical indicators vary and include, among others, chart formations, indexes, ratios, and gaps.

technically strong market: Term used when the markets as a whole are generally increasing in value on high volume.

technically weak market: Term used when the markets as a whole are generally declining in value on high volume.

technical move: A short fluctuation in the direction of a trend either up or down. This change can be seen as self-adjusting market movement.

technical rally: A rally in a period of general price declines. It does not reflect an improvement in overall fundamental conditions but rather bargain hunting or a self-adjustment. A technical rally rarely lasts more than a few weeks and is usually ended by profit taking.

technical research: *See* technical analysis.

technician: Person who uses a technical approach to analysis. One who is not concerned with the fundamentals of a company or the economy and bases predictions solely on technical chart patterns, ratios, and indexes.

tenants by the entirety: A joint owner-ship in a brokerage account or other property based on the marital status of the husband and wife. An account set up in this manner is permissible only in certain states.

tenants in common: A joint ownership in a brokerage account or other proper-ty in which each tenant has a divisible interest. *See* joint account (as tenants in common).

tender: To offer something of value to another person. In securities, it would be to offer stock to another person or to surrender one's shares for purchase by another.

tender offer: A public offer to buy all or a larger number of shares from existing shareholders of a corporation often at a price above current market price. The tender offer has a deadline date by which shares must be submit-ted.

10-K report: An annual report that all corporations with listed securities must file with the Securities and Exchange Commission.

term: The period of time until a bond or other debt obligations will mature.

term bond: A bond issue in which the entire issue matures on the same date. Term bonds typically have a sinking fund provision and may be callable.

testing: A market price that challenges the support or resistance levels with the expectation that the price will not fall below the support level or advance beyond the resistance level.

theory of contrary opinion: Market the-ory held by some that the majority is likely to be wrong when there is no real difference of opinion.

thinly held stock: Shares of a particular security are owned by relatively few individuals or institutions. This will result in wide price fluctuations on small volume.

thin market: A market in which there are relatively few bids to buy or offers to sell for a particular security. Price fluctuations are usually greater than when the market is more liquid. A thin market may result from lack of inter-est or from a limited number of shares for a particular issue.

third market: Trading of stock exchange listed securities off-the-board or in the over-the-counter market by nonmember brokers and investors. Many institutions buy and sell among themselves and often trades may be done off the floor if a large block would disrupt prices.

three against one ratio writing: A stock option ratio-writing strategy involving the sale of three calls for every 100 shares held of the underlying security.

ticker: The instrument that displays symbol, price, and volume information on security transactions within minutes after each trade. There are also news tickers that print the latest financial, corporate, market, and economic stories. *See* tape.

tick index: Net tick volume calculated by subtracting total downtick volume from total uptick volume on a particu-lar exchange for one trading session.

ticker tape symbol: Identifying letters assigned to a security. *See* symbol.

tick volume: Total downtick volume versus total uptick volume for a partic-ular security for one trading session.

tight money: A period when there is relatively little lendable money avail-able. It can result from government's attempt to slow inflation by using the various manipulative powers of the Federal Reserve.

time deposit: An interest-bearing deposit that cannot be withdrawn before a specified date without interest penalty.

time earnings: *See* price/earnings ratio.

time spread: A spread option strategy involving the purchase and sale of option contracts having the same striking price but different expiration dates. *Also called* calendar spread, horizontal spread.

time value: That portion of the premium on a stock option contract that reflects time remaining until expiration date. It is the amount by which the premium exceeds the intrinsic value.

timing: Judgment as to the best time to make additions to or deletions from one's portfolio of holdings according to secular, cyclical, and seasonal trends.

tip: Assumed "inside information" whether sound or just rumor regarding the affairs of a corporation that have not been released to the general public. A tip will often induce investors to buy or sell securities.

today only order: *See* day order.

tombstone: An announcement placed in various financial periodicals regarding a new security offering. It is not an offer to sell but is used only to indicate that the offering is or will be available and that interested investors should contact the underwriters.

top: The highest price a stock has reached during any given time period. The term can only be used in retrospect and must naturally be followed by a decline in market price. *Also called* peak.

topping out: Term used when a stock or market index has been advancing strongly for a period of time and then begins to moderate. There is an indication that a down-reversal will soon follow. The stock (or index) reaches a plateau or tops out and such a pattern may be considered a sell signal.

Toronto Stock Exchange: Address: 234 Bay Street, Toronto, Ontario, Canada M5J 1R1.

total return investment: An investment that offers a combination of income and growth with lessened capital risk.

tout: Highly biased recommendation to buy a stock.

trade: *See* transaction.

trade date: The day on which securities are bought or sold. The transaction date.

trader: An individual who buys and then sells securities within a short period of time in hopes of making short-term profits rather than seeking income or long-term growth.

traders' market: A general market condition in which it is possible to make short-term trades with the probability of making profits.

trading: Buying and selling securities in hopes of making short-term profits. Trading is less risky than speculating; however, it does involve more risk than long-term investing.

trading crowd: A number of members of a stock exchange gathered together at a trading post to transact buy and sell orders.

trading days: The days on which the securities exchanges are open. They are generally open Monday through Friday, except for certain holidays.

trading floor: The area of any stock exchange where security transactions actually take place. The NYSE has horseshoe-shaped trading posts where securities are traded. Only persons who hold a membership are allowed to trade on the floor of an exchange.

trading hours: Hours during which security transactions may take place on the floor of an exchange. Trading hours on the NYSE and AMEX are currently 10:00 a.m. to 4:00 p.m. EST Monday through Friday, except for certain holidays.

trading index: A market ratio that measures advances versus declines to upside versus downside volume. *See* short-term trading index.

trading instructions: Instructions (qualifier) given by an investor to the broker that in some way modify the standard buy or sell order. The most common trading instructions are: at the opening, at the close, not held, fill or kill, all or none, immediate or cancel, and the scale order.

trading post: Position on the floor of an exchange where trading for a particular security takes place.

trading range: The upper and lower limits of a security's price range. This range may be quoted either daily or for a longer period of time.

trading volume: The volume stated in number of shares, traded for a particular security, particular exchange, or market average or index for a given period of time. Generally, volume is quoted for a single trading day.

transaction: The execution of an order to buy or sell a stated number of shares of a particular security at market or limit price.

transaction slip: *See* confirmation slip.

transfer: (1) The legal conveyance of ownership from the seller to the buyer. (2) To record change in ownership in the corporate books.

transfer agent: The individuals or organizations that handle the physical transfer and recordkeeping of all transactions regarding stock of a corporation.

transfer tax: A federal and/or state tax imposed upon every stock transaction that is paid by the seller. The tax is extremely small and determined by the location of the transfer agent.

transportation index: *See* Dow Jones Transportation Average.

Treasury bill: Short-term debt instruments issued weekly by the U.S. Government on a discount basis with full face value due at maturity. T-bills are issued in denominations of $10,000 with income exempt from state and local income taxes. Maturities range from 91 to 182 and 359 days.

Treasury bond: Long-term debt instruments issued by the U.S. Treasury with maturity of ten years or longer. They are issued at par with semiannual interest payments being exempt from state and local taxes. Bonds and notes are quoted in points and thirty-seconds. A quote of 93.8 would equal 93 8/32 or $932.50.

Treasury note: Intermediate term-debt instruments issued by the U.S. Government with maturities of over one year and up to ten years. They are issued at par in denominations of $5,000 and $10,000 with interest payments semiannually being exempt from state and local taxes.

treasury stock: Stock that has been issued and then reacquired by the issuing corporation. While in the treasury of the corporation, it receives no dividends and has no voting rights.

trend: The longer term prevailing direction—advancing or declining—of price and/or volume movements.

trendline: A line that connects two or more points on a chart and represents the slope of movement. The line is connected between the lowest points or highest points and is used to indicate the direction a stock's price has been moving and to project future movements.

trickle-down theory: Economic theory stating that, rather than giving directly to consumers, it is better to give to businesses in order to induce economic growth which in turn will benefit the individual.

TRIN: *See* short-term trading index.

triple bottom: A charted price pattern that shows a stock has reached three substantial bottoms within a short period of time but is not going through the most recent bottom to a newer low price.

triple top: A charted price pattern that shows a stock has reached three substantial tops within a short period of time but is not going through the most recent top to a newer high price.

trough: Bottom or assumed bottom of economic activity.

trust: A legal arrangement whereby securities or other property is held by one person (the trustee) for the benefit of another person (the beneficiary).

trust company: An institution, usually a bank, that handles trusts and the investments in those trusts. Today most banks handle all trust-related functions.

trustee: A person or organization that has the legal responsibility for handling the property and investments of another person or organization.

Trust Indenture Act of 1939: Federal act that governs continuous disclosure by issuers of debt securities that are not covered under the Securities Act of 1933.

Truth in Securities Act: This act requires full disclosure of all material information regarding the public issuance of securities. *See* Securities Act of 1933.

turn: A change in market direction from down to up or vice versa.

turnaround situation: Situation where a company has moved from an unprofitable to a profitable position by solving its internal financial, management, processing, or marketing problems.

turnover: (1) The daily volume of securities traded on any given exchange. (2) The percentage of holdings in a portfolio that were bought and sold within a year.

two against one ratio writing: A stock option ratio-writing strategy involving the sale of two calls for every 100 shares held of the underlying security.

two-dollar broker: A member of an exchange who handles orders for other brokers who have more business than they can handle at a particular time. At

one time, two-dollar brokers were paid $2.00 for each 100-share lot they handled. Today two-dollar brokers are paid a fee based on the dollar value of the transaction.

two-way trade: Simultaneously selling out of one security and buying another so that investment dollars are not idle.

type of options: Term used in option transactions to indicate either a call option contract or a put option contract.

uncovered: A short option position for which the writer does not hold an offsetting, hedged position in the underlying security. *Also called* naked.

uncovered call writer: The writer (seller) of a call stock option contract who does not hold a hedged position in the underlying stock. *See* covered call writer.

uncovered option: A short stock option position for which the writer (seller) does not hold a hedged position in the underlying security. *Also called* naked option.

uncovered put writer: The writer (seller) of a put stock option contract who does not hold a hedged position in the underlying security. *See* covered put writer.

uncovered writer: The writer (seller) of a stock option contract who does not own shares or its equivalent of the underlying security. *Also called* naked option writer.

underlying security: The security for which a put or call option contract is written.

undervalued situation: Investment situation that exists when a particular security is depressed in price and justifies a higher current market value and price/earnings ratio.

underwriters: (1) The individuals or firms that guarantee certain obligations. (2) The individuals or groups who guarantee the sale of a new security offering by purchasing the entire issue and then offering it for sale to the public. Securities underwriters are often called investment bankers. The underwriters may also handle offerings on an all or none basis or on a best efforts basis.

underwriting: The process used to bring a new issue to the public market. One or more underwriters buy an issue outright from the issuer and then offer it for sale to the public. If the underwriters believe the market for the issue is uncertain they may accept the issue on a best efforts or on an all or none basis, thereby shifting the risk back to the issuing company.

underwriting spread: The dollar difference between the proceeds received by actual issuer in a public offering and the public offering price.

undivided account: One type of municipal securities underwriting in which each member of the syndicate has undivided selling and underwriting liability. *Compare* Western account, divided account. *Also called* Eastern account.

Uniform Gift to Minors Act: State laws that govern security transactions for minors and protect the interest of those minors.

unissued common stock: Authorized shares of common stock that have not yet been issued to shareholders. Unissued common stock differs from treasury stock and retired stock, both of which have been issued and then reacquired by the corporation.

United States Treasury issues: Debt instruments issued by the U.S. Government and backed by the full faith and credit of the government. The three principal U.S. Treasury securities are bills, notes, and bonds. The income they generate is exempt from state and local taxes, but not from federal income taxation.

unit investment trust: A diversified portfolio of income securities, for example corporate bonds, municipal bonds, or preferred stocks, which are pooled and sold to investors in the form of units. Each unit represents a fractional undivided interest in both the principal and income of the portfolio.

unit of trading: The number of shares that are normally handled as a unit. In stock trading, a unit of trading is typically 100 shares. However, a few issues are traded in 10, 25, or 50 share units.

unlisted option: A stock option contract that is not issued by the OCC and not traded on an organized options exchange, but rather is negotiated between the buyer and seller.

unlisted stock: Securities not listed with a registered stock exchange; for example, those securities traded in the over-the-counter markets.

unpaid dividend: A dividend that has been declared by a corporation but not yet paid to shareholders.

unrealized appreciation: An increase in the market value of a security above the price at which it was purchased. It is considered a paper profit rather than a realized profit until it is sold.

unrealized loss: A decrease in the market value of a security from the price at which it was purchased. It is considered a paper loss rather than a realized loss until it is sold.

unregistered stock: Stock issued on a limited basis for a special purpose or by smaller companies to a limited number of people within one state. The stock is not registered with the Securities and Exchange Commission. *See* letter stock.

unsecured debt: A debt obligation that is not backed by any collateral, but rather by the creditworthiness of the debtor.

unsubscribed shares: Shares in a securities offering that have not been sold by the underwriter to the public. Depending on the type of offering, these will be held by the underwriter for future sale, or the risk of unsold shares may rest with the issuing company.

upgrade: To sell out securities in a portfolio that are of a lower quality and replace them with higher-rated, high-quality securities.

up reversal: A sudden increase in price following a down trend. The term is used only to describe a short-term rise.

upside breakeven: The maximum upside price a security must advance before an investor begins to make a profit.

upside/downside volume ratio: The total number of shares traded that advanced divided by those that declined for a specified trading period or on a moving average basis.

upside potential: The degree of price appreciation that an investor or analyst believes a security is capable of obtaining. This potential price appreciation is usually based on both technical and fundamental projections.

upside trend: A period of prolonged advancing prices which may last up to several months. During this upside trend, there may be periods of down reversals.

uptick: A transaction that occurs at a higher price than the previous transaction. All short sales must be made on

an uptick or a zero plus tick. *Also called* plus tick. *Compare* downtick.

uptick/downtick block ratio: The number of NYSE blocks (excluding opening blocks) that traded on upticks divided by downtick blocks. Generally, a reading above 1.00 indicates an overbought condition while a reading below .40 can show an oversold condition.

up trend: A period when a security's prevailing price direction is upward.

value-added tax: Excise tax charged on the value that is added to a product at each state of production or on the production and distribution of a commodity.

Vancouver Stock Exchange: Address: 536 Howe Street, Vancouver, British Columbia, Canada V6C 2E1.

variable annuity: A life insurance product for which the premium is invested into a portfolio of securities in hopes that the value of the annuity will keep pace with inflation. When the contract is annuitized, the policyholder is paid based upon the accumulated dollar value of the security portfolio.

variable hedging: *See* ratio spreading.

variable income security: A security, usually common stock, whose dividend or yield is dependent upon the company's ability to make a profit. Income will vary from year to year or may not be paid at all.

variable ratio plan: One of several formula investing plans used to simplify the investing process. A portion of the investment capital is kept in common stock and the balance is placed in bonds or preferred stock. The proportions are varied according to general market changes.

variable spread: A stock option spread strategy involving the simultaneous purchase and sale of options on the same underlying security in which the number of contracts sold varies from the number of contracts purchased.

venture capital: Risk capital. The money invested in a new organization where the risk is decidedly higher than in a proven company.

vertical spread: A stock option spread strategy involving the simultaneous purchase and sale of options on the same underlying security having the same expiration months but different striking (exercise) prices. *Also called price spread.*

vested interest: An established right to an asset or right to a portion of an asset.

volatility: The extent to which price fluctuates in a short period of time. Highly volatile stocks show a greater degree of rapid and intense price changes.

volume: The total trading activity (number of shares traded) for a stock, group of stocks, or a market indicator for a specific time period. Volume figures are helpful in interpreting trends.

volume alert: A volume breakout that occurs when a security's volume or a market index volume exceeds its moving average for a specific period of time by some predetermined criteria.

voluntary plan: Program offered by most mutual funds under which an investor may purchase additional shares at any time. No limits are set on the number of shares purchased or on the time intervals between purchases.

voting rights: Shareholders, being the legal owners of a corporation, have the right to elect the board of directors and to vote on certain affairs of the corporation. This voting privilege may be delegated by means of a proxy. The positions, rights, and obligations of shareholders are protected by state security laws and the corporate charter.

voting stock: Stock that carries with it the collective voting privilege.

voting trust: Shareholders' assignment of their voting rights to a trustee for a limited period of time. The shareholders must abide by the decisions of the trustee.

voting trust certificate: A receipt for the common stock deposited with a trustee in a voting trust. It carries all rights granted except the right to vote.

Wall Street: This term is used in reference to the entire financial district in New York City, the main financial center of America. Wall Street, located in Manhattan, and the area surrounding it make up the financial community. *Also called* the Street.

Wall Street Journal: Highly regarded financial publication that concentrates on financial and market news. Address: Dow Jones & Co., Inc., 22 Cortland Street, New York, New York 10007.

warrant: A certificate issued by a corporation that represents an option to buy a stated number of shares of stock at a specific price on or before a specified date (a few are perpetual). Warrants have a value of their own and may be traded on the open market.

warrant value: The theoretical value of a warrant can be determined by subtracting the exercise price from the market price of the common stock and multiplying the sum by the number of shares that can be purchased with each warrant.

wash sale: (1) A sale of a security in which the loss is not allowed for tax purposes. A stock that is sold at a loss and repurchased within 30 days prior to or after that sale. To avoid a wash sale the investor may buy back the stock after the 30-day period or double up 31 days prior to the sale. (2) Buying and selling the same stock simultaneously through different brokers. If this leads to artificially increasing the trading volume and/or affecting the price, it is considered manipulation and is illegal.

wasting asset: An asset that decreases in real value over time. In securities, an investment that may decrease in value as it reaches an expiration date; for example, rights, warrants, and options.

watered stock: Stock that has been issued without adding a corresponding value to the corporate position.

weak market: A general decline in market prices for a relatively short period of time.

weekly sheets: Various lists published by the National Quotation Bureau that give market-makers and price quotations on over-the-counter securities. *See* pink sheets, white sheets, yellow sheets.

Western account: A syndication method in which each member of the underwriting syndicate is responsible only for its own allocation and not for any other member. *Also called* divided account. *Compare* Eastern account or undivided account.

when issued: Conditional transaction for an issue of securities that have been authorized for sale but not yet actually issued. Trading may begin on a when-issued basis which can last for several days to several weeks. After the security has been formally issued, trading will begin on a regular-way basis and final settlement takes place. *Also called* when, as, and if issued.

whipsawed: Losing on both sides of a price swing. For example, selling just before prices move up and then buying back just before they fall.

white knight: A corporation asked by a takeover candidate to bid for the takeover candidate in an attempt to keep an unwanted corporation from taking control. The white knight may replace the unwanted acquirer or just hinder the takeover process.

white sheets: A daily list published by the National Quotation Bureau that gives market-makers and price quotations for regional over-the-counter securities traded in Chicago, Los Angeles, and San Francisco.

Wholesale Price Index: Issued by the Bureau of Labor Statistics, this index measures price changes of goods sold at the wholesale level.

windfall: An unexpected gain. In investments, a sudden strong price ppreciation due to an unusual event, ch as a takeover announcement.

innipeg Stock Exchange: Address:)3-167 Lombard Avenue, Winnipeg, [anitoba, Canada R3B 0T6.

iped out: Losing all or nearly all of ne's investment.

ire house: Any member firm that aaintains communication systems ith its branch offices or correspond- it firms. Most brokerage firms today ould be considered wire houses ecause they operate branch offices aroughout the United States.

ithdrawal plan: A program available ith some mutual funds in which the vestor can request monthly or quar- rly distributions from the fund. The stribution may be limited to a fixed ite, or the dividends and/or capital ains received, or it may even exceed at rate.

ith interest: Indication in bond trans- ctions that the purchaser must pay to e seller all accrued interest from the st interest payment date up to but not cluding settlement date.

orking control: In theory it is the vnership of 51 percent or more of a rporation's voting stock. In practice, wever, if a stock is widely distribut- d, control can still be exerted with wer shares. *Also called* effective ntrol.

orkout market: A price stated for a curity that is not firm but rather a est estimate at the time it is given. milar to a subject price.

riter: The seller of a stock option con- act who has the obligation to buy or ll shares of the underlying security at predetermined price within a speci- ed period of time.

x: Symbol used in newspapers and financial periodicals to indicate that a stock is trading ex-dividend.

xd: Symbol used in newspapers and financial periodicals to indicate that a stock is trading ex-dividend.

xr: Symbol used in newspapers and financial periodicals to indicate that a stock is trading ex-rights.

xw: Symbol used in newspapers and financial periodicals to indicate that a stock is trading ex-warrants.

year-end dividend: A special or addi- tional dividend declared by the board of directors of a corporation at the end of the corporate fiscal year.

yellow sheets: Published daily by the National Quotation Bureau, these sheets list the market-makers and price quotations for over-the-counter corporate bonds.

yield: The return an investor receives on his investment. The annual dividends or interest received on securities. Yield is quoted as a percentage of current market price. *See* coupon yield, current yield, yield to maturity.

yield curve: Graphic expression of the relationship between yield and maturity.

yield spread: Comparison of yields offered on various issues of different quality.

yield to call: Yield to call measures the return on a bond investment an investor would receive stated as an average yearly return from purchase date to call date. Similar to yield to maturity.

yield to maturity: A measure of the average compounded yearly return on a bond based on acquisition price, maturity value, time to maturity, and coupon yield. This calculation takes into consideration all interest to be received from purchase date to maturity, plus or minus any discount or premium paid for the bond and redemption value at maturity.

zero basis: A measurement of yield. situation that occurs when a conver ble bond is selling at a premium great that the interest received is on equal to or less than the premium.

zero coupon bond: Just recently intr duced, these are corporate and gover ment bonds that are issued at a de discount from maturity value and pa no interest during the life of the bon they are redeemable at full face valu Tax consequences vary according the type of security, but typically th holder must declare the unpaid intere as ordinary income for tax purposes.

zero downtick: A transaction tha occurs at the same price as the prev ous transaction but lower than the la different price. *Also called* zero minu tick.

zero uptick: A transaction that occur at the same price as the previous tran saction but higher than the last differ ent price. *Also called* zero plus tick.

DIANNA B. CROWE is currently branch manager for Fidelity Investment in Sarasota, Florida. She was formerly a registered representative with Merrill Lynch Pierce Fenner & Smith in Atlanta, Georgia.

JAMES K. GLASSMAN, the publisher of *The New Republic,* has written extensively on personal finance for *The Atlantic Monthly, Forbes, The Washington Post* and many other magazines and newspapers.

WORLD ALMANAC PUBLICATIONS
200 Park Avenue
Department B
New York, New York 10166

Please send me, postpaid, the books checked below:

- ☐ THE WORLD ALMANAC AND BOOK OF FACTS 1985 . . . . $4.95
- ☐ THE WORLD ALMANAC EXECUTIVE APPOINTMENT BOOK 1985 . . $17.95
- ☐ THE WORLD ALMANAC BOOK OF WORLD WAR II $10.95
- ☐ THE WORLD ALMANAC DICTIONARY OF DATES $8.95
- ☐ THE LAST TIME WHEN $8.95
- ☐ WORLD DATA $9.95
- ☐ THE CIVIL WAR ALMANAC $10.95
- ☐ THE OMNI FUTURE ALMANAC $8.95
- ☐ THE LANGUAGE OF SPORT $7.95
- ☐ THE COOK'S ALMANAC $8.95
- ☐ THE GREAT JOHN L $3.95
- ☐ MOONLIGHTING WITH YOUR PERSONAL COMPUTER $7.95
- ☐ SOCIAL SECURITY & YOU: WHAT'S NEW WHAT'S TRUE $2.95
- ☐ KNOW YOUR OWN PSI-Q $8.95
- ☐ HOW TO TALK MONEY $7.95
- ☐ THE DIETER'S ALMANAC $7.95
- ☐ THE TWENTIETH CENTURY ALMANAC (hardcover) $24.95
- ☐ THE COMPLETE DR. SALK $8.95
- ☐ THE WORLD ALMANAC REAL PUZZLE BOOK. $2.95
- ☐ ABRACADABRA: MAGIC AND OTHER TRICKS (juvenile). $5.95
- ☐ CUT YOUR OWN TAXES & SAVE 1985 . . . . $2.95
- ☐ MIDDLE EAST REVIEW 1984 . . . . $24.95
- ☐ ASIA & PACIFIC 1984. . . . . $24.95
- ☐ LATIN AMERICA & CARIBBEAN 1984 . . . . $24.95
- ☐ AFRICA GUIDE 1984 . . . . $24.95

(Add $1 postage and handling for the first book, plus 50 cents for each additional book ordered.)

Enclosed is my check or money order for $_____

NAME_____

ADDRESS_____

CITY_____STATE_____ZIP_____